HOW YOU CAN FIND HAPPINESS

DURING THE

COLLAPSE

OF

WESTERN CIVILIZATION

HOW YOU CAN FIND HAPPINESS
DURING THE
COLLAPSE
OF
WESTERN CIVILIZATION

ROBERT J. RINGER

Published by QED

Distributed by
HARPER & ROW, PUBLISHERS
NEW YORK

Illustrations by Jack Medoff

Library of Congress Catalog Card No. 82-083446
ISBN 0-06-859606-5

TO MY MOTHER AND FATHER

who symbolize the best in Western Civilization, and who taught me, by way of example, its underlying morals and values.

Contents

CONTENTS

Preface

This book is something very different from its three predecessors. I quite literally felt a moral obligation to write *How You Can Find Happiness During the Collapse of Western Civilization*. At the risk of sounding melodramatic, it is, in truth, a book that *had* to be written.

Although in the beginning I fought the urge to become involved in an undertaking of this kind (pragmatism always stopped me cold), what finally motivated me to make a commitment to write the book were two conversations I had with major publishers. In the first of these conversations, the head of a paperback house said to me, "Forget the doom-and-gloom stuff. Those books were good last year, but next year it will be something different—yoga, diets, animal care, or what have you. These things come and go in cycles."

I was dumbfounded! I couldn't believe that this well-educated, intelligent executive had absolutely no idea of what was happening in the Western world. He had become so numb to the increasing chaos he had for years been witnessing that it no longer registered with him in any meaningful way. To him, crisis was just a fad—no more or no less important than a hundred other cocktail-party topics. After considerable effort, I tired of trying to explain to him that "gloom and doom" was an irresponsible epithet for the honest disclosure of some very real and serious problems, and that those problems were *not* going to go out of vogue like diets, mini skirts, or hoola hoops.

The second conversation, which proved to be the crowning blow, was with a hardcover publisher. It was just after Ronald Reagan's election that this publisher said to me, "You're making a big mistake. With Reagan in office, there are going to be major changes in Washington, which means major changes throughout the country. What if unemployment is down to 5% by the time your book comes out? What if interest rates are down to 8% and the economy is booming?"

At first, I honestly thought he was kidding. I have such a narrow circle of acquaintances, all of whom are very much in touch with the realities of today's world, that I often forget that most people are living in a dream world. Alas, this gentleman was *not* kidding. He really believed that the Demopublican's latest white knight was going to make significant changes. He really believed that, even if a president were willing to *try* to do the right thing, he would have the *power* to do it.

Again, here was a supposedly well-educated, intelligent executive of a large corporation who was totally out of touch with reality. He apparently had no understanding of the metamorphosis that was taking place not only in the United States, but in all Western nations. Certainly he had no understanding of the underlying causes of this metamorphosis. Like the first publisher, he also believed that "that doomsayer stuff tends to come and go in cycles."

Were it not for these two publishers, this book might never have been written. That being the case, I'm not sure whether to curse or thank them. On the one hand, it was the most difficult project of my life, and on more than one occasion I regretted having been so stubborn as to undertake it. On the other hand, now that the task has been completed, I must admit that I am happy I was aroused to the point of doing so.

In a sense, if this book helps just one straight-thinking individual in the Western world to improve his life, it will have been worth the effort. Hopefully, that individual will be you.

— *Robert J. Ringer*
April 1, 1983

SECTION
I

APOCALYPSE
NOW

CHAPTER I

Fun and Sun
at the
Ice Cream Stand

It was early in the afternoon of a hot summer's day. I was standing in line at a neighborhood ice cream stand, with five or six people in front of me and about the same number lined up at an adjacent window. As we stood quietly waiting our turns, a rather unpleasant mix of screeching musical instruments, wailing voices, and sharp electronic pulses began to fill the air.

As I and the other patrons in line turned to see what all the ruckus was about, the intrusive sounds were practically upon us. Crossing the street and heading straight for the ice cream stand was a scraggly-looking teenager, sporting one of those now-familiar "I'm a bad dude" looks on his face. As if his gait and demeanor weren't menacing enough, he was also armed with the ultimate punk weapon—a "portable" radio that, considering its size, would have fit rather comfortably in the right hand of Godzilla.

As Mr. Bad Dude sauntered up and attached himself to the adjacent line, the discordant "rock" sounds blaring from his gigantic noise machine became more than just mildly irritating. Then, a most interesting thing happened. Just as I was expecting him to do the natural and civilized thing—turn the radio down so as not to annoy the other people in line—he startled everyone by deliberately turning his rock blaster *up*.

3

The message was clear: "I can do whatever the hell I want. You don't like it? Tough s____, man. I'm bad."

All at once, it hit me. He was right. He *could* do whatever he wanted, and if I didn't like it, that was my tough luck. Yet that arrogant punk, that "bad dude," made me recognize something that had eluded me up to that time.

For years I had been amazed at the gritty tenacity of Western Civilization. It seemed incredible to me that it had endured in the face of one crisis after another, that it had withstood blow after blow without totally collapsing. Now, for the first time, I understood why. The much-heralded collapse of Western Civilization was not an event that was going to take place all at once on some specific future date. The "collapse" was an *ongoing* phenomenon, an event that would take place over a long period of time—at least decades, and perhaps centuries. Suddenly I understood that everyone who had been waiting for the long-predicted collapse to occur would wait a long time indeed, for the collapse had long since begun! Because such people have erroneously assumed that the collapse would manifest itself as one momentous, cataclysmic event, they have been oblivious to the fact that it has not only been in progress for decades, but is rapidly *accelerating* before their very eyes.

At that tense moment at the ice cream stand, it occurred to me that what I was witnessing in that repugnant teenager's rude behavior was the literal destruction of the most civilized way of life the world has ever known, a way of life that evolved over a period of several centuries in western Europe, the United States, and a number of other countries whose roots were chiefly European. (Although in recent decades much has been written about the "Westernization" of such Eastern nations as Japan, this is more descriptive of the effects of industrialization than it is of a centuries-old ethic or way of life.) Collectively, these countries have come to be loosely referred to as "the West," "Western Civilization," or "the Occident."

At its zenith, the Western way of life encompassed a unique blend of beliefs, characteristics, principles, and philosophies.

Numbered among its virtues were honesty, self-discipline, non-violence, self-sufficiency, the work ethic, respect for elders, aggrandizement of achievement, planning for the future, respect for the property of others, a stable economic system, reverence for the family unit, courtesy and consideration toward others, and, above all, the right of the individual to be left alone. When I speak of the collapse of Western Civilization, then, it is the literal destruction of this way of life that I am referring to.

Certainly, Mr. Bad Dude would have been gratified to know that at that moment he served as a vivid symbol of the dispossession of Western virtues, living proof that the deterioration of a once-great civilization was already well under way. Yet I seriously doubt that anyone else who witnessed the same scene on that hot summer afternoon assigned such historic importance to the event, even though by now the manifestations of the collapse are everywhere. Mr. Bad Dude's theatrics at the ice cream stand represent but one small example from among a large body of persuasive evidence:

—Approximately 5,000 teenagers in the United States commit suicide each year. That's thirteen per day! Since 1960 the number of suicides in the 15-to-24 age bracket has more than doubled, while the incidence of suicide among children in the 10-to-14 age group has increased by 32% since as recently as 1976.

—The prime interest rate, once thought to be out of control at 8%, has already reached 21½% (and will go much higher in the not-too-distant future, as will be explained later in this book).

—U.S. automakers cry to Congress, demanding laws that would force Americans to buy their inferior automobiles at higher prices than they would have to pay for better automobiles made in other countries.

—In the Miami riots of 1980, rioters destroyed some $245 million worth of property. Before it was over, fifteen people were killed and hundreds injured. The result? A groveling Jimmy Carter, then president of the United States, virtually *apologized to the rioters* as he sent one government official after another to Miami to assure them that their "grievances" would be satisfied.

—The savings and loan industry teeters on the brink of bankruptcy, with the Federal Savings and Loan Insurance Corporation paying out more money to financially troubled savings and loans in the past few years than it paid out *in its previous forty-six years of existence combined.* Worse, savings and loan companies continue to run ads that proclaim that putting money into a savings account is "risk free," while the general public is unaware that the FSLIC does not have enough funds to cover even 1% of the potential losses of savers.

—The National Labor Relations Board recently overturned the ten-day suspension of a Honeywell worker who had smeared graffiti in the men's lavatory, maintaining that his defacement of someone else's property was an acceptable "public airing of his grievance."

—Movies like "Fame" and "Saturday Night Fever," whose primary artistic coup seems to be that their characters are able to inundate audiences with more vulgar words and gestures per minute than was thought possible (or necessary) during more stable times, are met with enthusiastic approval from moviegoers. In the movie "Grease," a huge box office success, the heroine delights the audience by shedding her nice-girl image and—just in time to bring about a "happy" ending—becoming a tramp!

—Drugs circulate freely, not just in society in general, but in high schools and elementary schools as well. Sources have estimated that as many as 50% of the players in the National Football League, often role models to the young, use cocaine.

—The concept of punishing winners and rewarding losers now goes virtually unchallenged: The U.S. Senate in one week saw fit to *penalize* the oil industry with a $178 billion tax for having *succeeded* in making profits, while at the same time *rewarding* Chrysler Corporation with $1.5 billion in loan guarantees for having *failed* to the tune of $1 billion.

—Confused, directionless children flock to back-alley clubs where alienated weirdos in bizarre dress entertain them by breaking props and "singing" about such things as oral sex, sadism, violence, and drugs.

—In New York City, persons earning up to 80% of the median income for that area can qualify for "housing for the poor" that includes, in one instance, an apartment building with parquet floors, individually controlled heating and air conditioning, balconies, plus access to tennis courts and swimming pool. Tenants apply 15% to 25% of their income toward the rent, which can easily exceed $1,000 per month, while taxpayers are forced to foot the bill for the balance.

—With sexual promiscuity now accepted among all classes of society, one of every ten girls between the ages of 15 and 19 becomes pregnant each year—more than one million girls annually.

—Each year we save less and consume more. In fact, we have become a full-fledged credit-card society in which most people spend more than they actually earn. In the United States, the result is that personal debt has risen from $228.2 billion in 1960 to well over $1.5 *trillion* today, and, as with government debt, can never be repaid.

The list is as long as you care to make it. All one needs to do is read his local newspaper and observe what is going on around him every day. Most of corporate America is in financial trouble. Teenage gangs run rampant; no longer satisfied with just killing each other, they have begun to roam affluent areas and kill people simply for the sport of it. No one wants to work anymore—just try to find a plumber or an electrician who is pleasant, takes pride in his work, and is available when you need him. The majority of workers, well versed in all the coercive laws protecting workers' "rights," instantly drop whatever they are working on when lunch or quitting time arrives and quickly disappear. The movie industry is concerned because people are finally beginning to boycott movie theaters in response to the increasing noise level and general rudeness of a growing number of patrons. Professional athletes routinely demand that their contracts be renegotiated after a good year, despite their *already* being legally bound by an existing contract (and despite their mysterious reluctance to renegotiate *downward* after a *bad* year). Lightly beeping your horn at another driver has become a dangerous act, often leading to threats, violence, or even death. It is rare to find a phone booth that hasn't had its telephone books stolen, its door destroyed, and its telephone rendered inoperative. It almost takes an act of God to get a salesperson to wait on you in a retail store, and even God can't make him be nice to you. Strikes by militant garbage collectors occur more and more frequently, choking major cities in an unbearable stench, but leading to the emergence of a new middle class of high-paid garbage collectors.

Perhaps worst of all, the very cornerstone of Western Civilization, the family unit, has rapidly disintegrated. Parents have learned that they need not be concerned with their child's problems, because the government will take care of him. Beginning with the day he starts school and receives his first "free" government lunch, a child is taught to look to the government, not his family, for solutions to his problems. In another Western country, Sweden, the government recently passed a law making it illegal for parents to punish a child by spanking him or "humiliating" him in any way—such as by preventing him from talking to his friends! With the very core of Western society, the family unit, relinquishing its place of eminence in the lives of most people, it is no wonder that adults in all walks of life—from waitresses to retail clerks, from repairmen to airline ticket agents—are increasingly disrespectful, rude, and hostile.

How did conditions in the Western world get so out of hand? Through a very clever process known as *gradualism*. Gradualism is a remarkable technique, particularly when applied to human beings, for the empirical evidence clearly shows that man does not respond well to abrupt change. On the other hand, he has proved to be extremely malleable when subjected to gradual change over long periods of time.

This point has not been lost on the enemies of individual liberty. It is to their credit that they have had the good sense to be patient. They have been pragmatic enough to realize that one does not turn the world upside down in a fortnight. One rotates it slowly so that those on its surface scarcely notice they are moving.

Through the application of gradualism, people ultimately come to accept change as the status quo. Ideally, a way of life that would have been considered enslavement by one generation is regarded as freedom by a later generation that grows up never knowing any other kind of existence. So it has been with the collapse of Western Civilization; it is a testimony to the effectiveness of gradualism. People have become accustomed to a world in crisis. They do not see the decadence and financial chaos that surround them as evidence of a collapse. At most, they look to the *future* and ponder when a collapse might occur. Few people, however, believe that such a collapse is even possible.

A collapse, by its very nature, gains momentum as it proceeds. The decline of the West can be illustrated by a graph that accelerates exponentially, so that, in the case of the United States, more evidence of the collapse can be seen in the fifty years between 1913 and 1963 than in the previous 137 years; and more evidence can be seen in the past twenty years than in the previous fifty. There is no question that the slope of the collapse's trendline is becoming steeper each year.

The situation can no longer be passed off with the traditional ostrich retort, "Aw, there've always been problems. The problems are no worse now than they were in my parents' time." Anyone who is at least thirty years old knows better, providing he has been *awake* during those thirty years, because he has been witnessing, firsthand, the reality that the problems *are* getting worse, as well as increasing in number, at an accelerating rate.

Ironically, a primary impetus behind this rapid acceleration is that most people do not even want to acknowledge that anything is wrong. Their logic is quite extraordinary: Somehow, if one just refuses to think about it, everything will turn out all right.

CHAPTER II

The Legalization
of Lynching

An important distinction must now be emphasized. It is often said that sexual promiscuity, drugs, violence, financial chaos, and other modern ills are themselves responsible for the deterioration of Western society, but such a view is erroneous. The sampling of disturbing attitudes and behaviors catalogued in the preceding chapter are not *causes* of the collapse of Western Civilization; rather, they are *symptoms*—clear evidence that the collapse is, in fact, well under way.

But symptoms are only manifestations of an underlying disorder. To achieve happiness and success, you must have the vision to look beyond symptoms to causes. What is the fundamental *reason* behind the collapse of Western Civilization?

For most people, the cause of the collapse is more difficult to perceive than the collapse itself. The *symptoms* of the collapse are clearly visible to everyone; the *cause,* however, is subtle, almost hidden from the mind of the average person who relies on the media to do his thinking for him. The cause of the collapse of Western Civilization can be traced to a full-scale *revolution*.

Even the most extreme "alarmists" among us do not really grasp what has happened. While it's true that such alarmists often insist that a "revolution" is coming, such a revolution, much

11

to the delight of the we-told-you-so media, never quite makes its appearance. And with good reason. The revolution is not *coming;* like the collapse itself, the revolution has *already arrived.* Unlike the collapse, however, the revolution is *over.*

How can this be? Very simple. It came and went while Americans were watching Monday Night Football, sipping their bottles of Miller Lite, and stuffing themselves with Big Macs. They simply ignored the whole event, because to comprehend it would require thinking. And thinking takes effort. Of course, it was easy to ignore, because it was a quiet revolution. It was, in fact, a *moral revolution.* And it was the success of this moral revolution that was the moving force—the *cause*—behind the collapse of Western Civilization.

In a very literal sense, the moral standards of a civilization constitute its foundation. (When I use the word *moral,* I am talking about a standard of behavior that forms a system of ethics—i.e., principles of conduct—for an individual or group. Therefore, what is considered moral at any given time among any group of people will vary widely.) When the foundation is destroyed, the civilization itself—the very structure—must fall. At worst, the civilization may disappear entirely; at best, a new civilization, with a new system of ethics, will displace the fallen one.

The moral revolution that undermined our own civilization involved a 180-degree shift in the generally accepted standards of behavior, or principles of conduct, for the people of Western nations. Gradually, some of the most cherished values and beliefs of yesterday have come to be considered immoral, while some of the worst vices of the past are now accepted and even encouraged. As a result, we now live in a world turned upside down, which means that most people today are—morally speaking—standing on their heads!

An enormous upheaval like the one we've undergone must begin very slowly if it is to have any chance of succeeding. As I pointed out, that is the beauty of gradualism: the citizenry is never jolted to the point of threatening armed rebellion. Instead, as one generation passes on and another grows up in its place, the

*"Whaddaya mean you're interruptin' da game to tell me dat
Western Civilization's collapsin'? I'm gonna write my
congressman!"*

creeping changes become the status quo. Anyone who challenges the new status quo is, of course, labeled unpatriotic, anarchistic, or just plain crazy.

At the very heart of the moral disintegration of Western Civilization was the shift from the sacrosanct belief in individual rights to a belief in lynch-mob rule (better known as "majority rule"). In other words, "right" became whatever the most powerful alliance of people at any given time said it was. (Whether you call such an alliance "the populace," "the people," or "the mob" is quite irrelevant.) In a democracy, this concept is defended on the grounds that it guarantees "that which is best for the greatest number of people." In point of fact, however, the notion that one group of people has a right to commit aggression against another group, based on the premise that "the majority is always right" (translation: might is right), is without moral justification.

In early America, this procedure was called by its proper name—"lynching." If a group decided, rightly or wrongly, that someone was deserving of its wrath, it simply used brute force to do whatever it pleased to that individual. Such action was illegal, of course, because it was done without government sanction. *That was the key—government sanction!* And it was the granting of that ultimate sanction that was the catalyst for the moral revolution. It paved the way for lynch-mob rule, or so-called majority rule, to displace individual sovereignty as the moral underpinning of Western Civilization.

The practical problem with "majority rule" is that a political democracy is too fragile to withstand the greed and envy of men. Inevitably, greedy and envious people—both voters and politicians—begin to figure out how to use so delicate a system to their advantage. Voters test the waters and, much to their delight, find that they can plunder their neighbors simply by voting to change the laws that were originally set up to protect lives and property. Politicians, of course, figure out relatively early that they can achieve political longevity by appealing to voters' greed and envy, since everyone possesses these negative traits to one degree or another.

"Quiet, baldy. I represent the majority, and they don't like green reptiles."

In the early stages of the moral revolution, only hard-core nonproducers (politicians, thieves, and the terminally shiftless) fully understood the possible implications of a political democracy. With each passing year, however, more and more producers caught on to the game and went the way of the nonproducers. That is to say that basically honest, hard-working people ultimately gave in to their human weaknesses and elected to fulfill their desires through the ballot box instead of through productive labor.

This caused a natural acceleration in the evolution of both the revolution and the collapse. As more and more people surrendered to their ignoble instincts, they increasingly fought one another for control of the lynching apparatus (i.e., the legislative process). This in turn whetted the politician's appetite for power, because he could see, clearly and tantalizingly, that the promise to use his legislative machinery to lynch every citizen's neighbor would bring him the necessary votes to attain and hold public office. It was then but a small step to the next revolutionary plateau: the "anything-goes society."

How does an anything-goes society work? First, man is a creature of infinite desires, all of which he wishes to see fulfilled. He is clever enough to realize, however, that merely saying that he "wants" something is not likely to procure it for him, especially if he is dependent upon someone else to provide it. How much better to claim that the thing he desires is something he truly "needs." And that is the key to an anything-goes society: the proper manipulation of an innocent-sounding little four-letter word, *need*.

Need is perhaps the cleverest word ever adopted by thieves and powermongers. Through the use of this seemingly harmless word, *all* acts of aggression can be morally justified. The overriding rule of the anything-goes game is that a need is deemed valid so long as the mob says it is; i.e., the majority is magically omniscient when it comes to determining who is "in need."

What is conveniently forgotten is that the majority's decision is subjective; i.e., it is but an opinion. There is, of course, no such thing as an absolute need. I may think I "need" a Rolls Royce; you may think I "need" a bicycle. Neither of us is right or wrong. It is just a difference of opinion.

But my *desire* for a Rolls Royce is another matter. There is no opinion involved there. If I *desire* a Rolls Royce, that's *my* business. It only becomes your business if I arbitrarily decide that you have an obligation to buy it for me, on the grounds that it is a "need" and that I am therefore "entitled" to it. The fact that I may call my desire for a Rolls Royce a "need" is transparent poppycock. I may just as well call it a wart. No matter what word I assign to it, I still have no moral right to force you to help me acquire it just because I happen to want it.

Unfortunately, that is not how the majority of people now see the matter. Through the gradual evolution of lynch-mob rule, fueled by the titanic forces of media-induced guilt and envy, the word *need* has successfully emerged as a camouflage for individual desire. But this camouflage is *not* the final step in the evolutionary process. The complete emergence of an anything-goes society ultimately comes about through the remarkable elevation of "needs" to "rights."

And that is precisely where we stand today. We are now a society whose people believe that every individual has a *right* to a "free" education, a *right* to a "minimum" wage, a *right* to "free" medical care, a *right* to "decent" housing, a *right* to virtually anything that he can establish as "society's obligation" to him, whereas we were once a society whose people believed that no one had a right to *anything* except life, liberty, and the pursuit of his own happiness.

As alien as it may now sound, most of our great-grandparents, and even a good number of our grandparents and parents, actually believed, before the moral revolution was won, that each individual had the right to keep *everything* he earned and the right to be left alone. (As might be expected, people were more favorably inclined toward charity then—charities of *their choice,* that is—but charity was recognized as a matter of personal morality, to be decided by each individual.) Now, by contrast, talk of individualism is quickly dismissed as impractical or unrealistic in a "complex world." In a sense, this is the ultimate triumph of gradualism—that our culture has reached the stage where freedom is actually considered to be unrealistic!

Thus, our civilization has evolved to the point where the use of force and fraud can be easily justified on the grounds that such measures are necessary to make certain that people's "rights" are not violated (i.e., to make certain that their individual desires are fulfilled). And that is the bottom line of an anything-goes society—the *moral acceptance* of the use of any means necessary to satisfy individual desires.

There is, quite obviously, one glaring problem with this otherwise beautiful piece of nonlogic. In order to fulfill the "rights" of one person, someone else's rights must be violated, because any product or service that an individual may desire must be produced by someone else. And if the product or service (or the money to purchase it) is taken from the productive citizen against his will, then *his* rights are sacrificed to the desires of the person who receives the largess.

Through the not-so-discreet use of majority rule, however, individual rights can simply be ignored. This comes about through continual redefinition of the political democracy, until it finally becomes a legal mechanism for implementing force and fraud. Government, in effect, takes on the role of a hired gun for the plunderers. And who are the plunderers? Frederic Bastiat gave us some insight:

> When plunder is organized by law for the profit of those who make the law, all the plundered classes try somehow to enter—by peaceful or revolutionary means—into the making of laws. According to their degree of enlightenment, these plundered classes may propose one of two entirely different purposes when they attempt to attain political power: Either they may wish to stop lawful plunder, or they may wish to share in it.

The problem, of course, is that the majority of people are not at all enlightened, thus they quite naturally choose to *share* in the plunder. Further, the typical false-prosperity addict *does not want to be enlightened.* He is too busy enjoying his $15,000 home (for which he paid $125,000), his state-of-the-art stereo system and two television sets (which he is paying off over three years at the legal-limit interest rate), and his new swimming pool (financed by a second mortgage on his already overpriced home). "Enough of this nonsense that Western Civilization is collapsing," says he. "Let the good times roll."

This popular preference for fiction over fact draws me to the conclusion that someday historians will look back and note with curiosity that, as Western Civilization slipped quietly down the moral drain, no one particularly noticed. They were not enlightened enough to understand that to take part in the plunder even passively, rather than put an end to it, was only in their *short-term* best interest. They were not able to comprehend that in the long term, as a result of the crumbling of their political democracy, even the cleverest of the plunderers would lose. Thus, they evolved into a massive "voting class," whose objective was to gain control of the lynching mechanism.

Each person, organization, and company now claims to qualify in some way as "truly needy," a term that is conveniently undefinable but extremely intimidating. After all, who but a cold and heartless individual would deny the truly needy their "rights"? And so the mass thefts in our desires-are-rights society are carried out under the grand farce of euphemistic labels— "humanitarianism," "sensitivity to the needs of others," or just plain "reform."

This immoral madness has by now escalated into an avalanche of government "social programs" that not even the most ardent socialist could have hoped for fifty years ago. For example, in 1962 there were 151,000 people on food stamps at a cost of $14.1 million; by 1980, the figures had risen to 22.5 million people and $11.3 billion. In 1936, there were 534,000 people collecting $21.3 million under the Aid to Families with Dependent

Children program; by 1980, the figures had risen to 11 million people and $7 billion. In just the ten years between 1970 and 1980, the cost of school-lunch programs increased from $400 million to $4 billion, Medicaid and Medicare allotments increased from $9.9 billion to $47.8 billion, housing "assistance" increased from $500 million to $5.3 billion, Social Security payments increased from $29.7 billion to $117.9 billion, unemployment insurance increased from $3.7 billion to $15.6 billion, and federal employees' retirement benefits increased from $2.7 billion to $14.3 billion. *The unenlightened masses have, indeed, chosen to plunder!*

A majority of these thefts are accomplished through a variety of taxes, particularly the graduated income tax, which didn't even come into existence until 1913, and only then by "amending" the Constitution. This piece of legislation (the Sixteenth Amendment) in effect amended the Eighth *Commandment,* which used to state, "Thou shalt not steal." Politicians, urged on by covetous voters, simply decided to amend God, as follows: "Thou shalt not steal, unless thou hast a 'need' for something, and then only by using the force of government to accomplish thy theft."

Aside and apart from open theft via taxation, the government, in its desperation to raise more funds to keep up with its political-plunder promises, resorts to fraud. And the most successful fraud, the one yielding the greatest return at the least amount of political risk, is the creation of paper money.

While holders of paper currency were no doubt startled when Franklin Roosevelt confiscated their gold in 1933, gradualism eventually won out. A new and "socially enlightened" generation has come to accept paper money as real money, perhaps not even realizing that paper dollars were only supposed to be IOU's for real money (i.e., gold). They have all but forgotten that the gold itself was stolen by Uncle Sam.

Today, however, as many hard-money analysts have correctly pointed out, dollars are really "IOU-Nothings." The evolution is quite easy to follow. The 1928 "dollar" bore the following inscription: "The United States of America will pay to the bearer on demand one dollar. Redeemable in gold on demand at the United States Treasury." By 1963, the inscription on the "dollar" had been changed to read: "This note is legal tender for all debts public or private." Translation: This piece of paper is money because the government says it is. Note that when the dollar was backed by gold, it was not necessary for the government to state that it was "legal tender."

The creation of this IOU-Nothing money is called *monetary inflation* (i.e., an increase in the amount of money in circulation). By injecting greater and greater doses of fiat currency into the economy, more and more money is made available to *some* people, and they use this newly created money to bid for the same goods and services as people who actually earn their money. This bidding causes a chain reaction that forces prices and wages up throughout the economy, *at an uneven pace,* and it is this increase in prices that most people commonly refer to as "inflation." The latter, however, should more technically be labeled *price inflation.*

Again, the slumbering public is kept sedated through a daily stream of intentional disinformation that ignores the distinction between monetary inflation (the cause) and price inflation (the result). People hear only about "inflation" (inflation of what?) and follow the government's wild-goose chases in search of the evil entity that is causing it. Needless to say, the cause has never been tracked down by any government.

The attractiveness of this kind of theft is that, unlike direct taxation, it is an *invisible* theft. When people begin to get restless because of high taxes, monetary inflation is a way for government to steal without taxpayers being aware of it. Best of all, monetary inflation provides the government with endless scapegoats as it frantically pretends to "fight inflation."

Finally, politicians have learned how to buy votes by passing laws that allow for subtle thefts by individuals and companies without the use of government as a middleman. Thus, a person has a *right* to receive a higher wage than his employer would voluntarily pay him; he has a *right* to buy fuel at a lower price than a company would voluntarily sell it to him for; he has a *right* to rent an apartment at a lower cost than the owner of the apartment building would voluntarily rent it for. In an anything-goes society, he has a "right" to virtually anything anyone else produces at a price that *he* wants to pay for it.

In such a morally bankrupt environment, where the government's use of force and fraud has achieved moral credibility, it is certainly understandable why a civilization disintegrates. As pointed out earlier, once the moral foundation of a society shifts (in the case of Western Civilization, from individual sovereignty to group-force rule), it is not possible for the societal structure supported by that foundation to remain unchanged.

Once people know that the fruits of their labor can be taken from them by force, and that the theft will be accepted as a moral action, then the gates to an anything-goes nightmare swing open. Once the use of force and fraud to achieve one's ends is not only condoned, but encouraged, the moral dominoes quickly begin to fall. It then becomes easy to give a moral stamp of approval to virtually any other action previously thought to be immoral or obscene. If one vice is acceptable, why not another, and another, and another? It is then only a matter of time until all other standards and values begin to crumble.

So it is not by accident that we are surrounded by madness and contradiction. It is not by accident that today's young people savor the barbaric sounds of punk rock, sounds produced by depraved, pitiful souls who in earlier times would have been looked upon as the dregs of society. It is not by accident that drugs and explicit sex are to be found everywhere. It is not by accident that violence is the order of the day. These phenomena are predictable hallmarks of an anything-goes society.

Encouraged by the might-is-right philosophy of lynch-mob rule, people have come to believe that they have a right to be rewarded just for being alive. In such an atmosphere, hard work and honesty become passé. The natural consequence of this kind of thinking is a total disregard for life and property, which is, above all, reflected in the rapidly accelerating problem of teenage crime. The most recently published figures show that 31% of all those arrested for violent crimes and 54% of those arrested for property crimes are teenagers. The philosophy is: "If you want something, you have a right to take it."

Though moral bankruptcy was the spiritual force behind Western Civilization's demise, it is the resultant *fiscal* bankruptcy of Western nations that has emerged as the dominant *physical* force behind the collapse. The fiscal problems caused by the desires-are-rights stampede of voters have now taken on a life of their own. As each new generation grows up under the umbrella of the desires-are-rights morality, desires tend to increase. From elementary school through college, government-educated and government-paid instructors "help" young minds to make the necessary transition from desires to "needs" to "rights."

The process thus becomes self-perpetuating. As more and more young adults come to accept desires as rights, and as each person's desires continue to increase, ever greater amounts of wealth must be taken from productive people to fulfill them. Obviously, this motivates still more people to become increasingly "needy" and less productive, so the cycle continually worsens.

All the force and fraud government can bring to bear is not enough to appease a society that has reached the anything-goes stage. When politicians can no longer satisfy all of the demands of voters, those voters grow indignant and protest that their "rights are being violated." The kind of people who in previous decades were poor and humble are now poor and *militant*.

As the situation deteriorates, desperate people become savvy enough to group themselves together—the elderly, small businessmen, blacks, rent-control advocates, Mexican-Americans, "the poor," even the handicapped. Each group becomes more and more hostile as it demands that its "rights" be guaranteed—i.e., that government force be used against other members of society to fulfill the group's desires.

At that point, lynch-mob rule is out of control, because each group insists that the lynching apparatus be used on *its* behalf.

Politicians, once so enamored of the desires-are-rights ruse, are increasingly at a loss for solutions. As productivity rapidly decreases and demands continue to increase, there is simply not enough to go around. With everyone clamoring for the government to lynch everyone else, the hierarchy of the political structure implements the only possible solution available to it: It lynches everyone!

It isn't that the government is adept at decisive action; it's simply that it has no other choice. As people's desires fail to be met, they panic; they become hysterical; finally, they resort to violence. As the situation deteriorates, either the existing government steps in and imposes martial law or a new government will arise to suppress the social chaos.

Unfortunately, there is overwhelming historical evidence that when the social order completely breaks down, when anarchy and pandemonium reign, both citizens and elected officials not only yield to dictatorial power, they welcome it. Comments to that effect were common during the Great Depression. The governor of Kansas, Alf Landon, opined that "Even the iron hand of a national dictator is in preference to a paralytic stroke." Senator David Reed of Pennsylvania was even more specific: "If this country ever needed a Mussolini, it needs one now."

Thus the rise to power of Franklin D. Roosevelt, whose dictatorial reach, during far better times than we will soon experience, encompassed an expanse not dreamed possible just a few years earlier. In Germany, during the same period, Hitler used social chaos as the excuse to implement a permanent police state, which was *hailed* by millions of weary, frightened, and confused Germans. The same scenario has been replayed time and again throughout the centuries. History repeats itself, because human nature genetically repeats itself generation after generation.

Austrian economist and Nobel laureate F. A. Hayek explains man's stubborn attraction to self-deception this way: "It seems almost as if we did not want to understand the development which has produced totalitarianism because such an understanding might destroy some of the dearest illusions to which we are determined to cling."

Unbeknownst to all but a handful of Americans, the machinery to implement a police state is already in place in the United States. It exists in the form of an unpublicized little piece of "legislation" called Executive Order 11490. It gives the president the right to invoke emergency powers in "any national emergency-type situation." Of course, it is the president himself who *decides* what constitutes an emergency. Once he has activated 11490, the president can do virtually *anything* he deems "necessary," including confiscating gold, silver, and firearms, nationalizing businesses, controlling the media, freezing bank accounts, censoring mail, forcing you to "share" your possessions with others, and preventing citizens from leaving the country.

Where Western Civilization goes from that point—well, your guess is as good as mine. Neither of us can exercise a great deal of control over the outcome, but we can, to a great extent, control our *own* outcomes. And that's what this book is all about.

CHAPTER III

The Good News

Now for some perspective. Notwithstanding the sobering observations I have expressed up to this point, the fact is that the end of Western Civilization is *not* the end of the world.

All the great civilizations of history have had beginnings and ends. The nature of life is cyclical. The empires of Byzantium, Spain, the United Kingdom, Greece, and Rome have all come and gone. Interestingly, however, life relentlessly transcends revolution and collapse. It has developed a fascinating habit of continuing on, despite the fact that most of history, as Voltaire pointed out, has been "no more than the portrayal of crimes and misfortunes."

The point is that life in all of these fallen empires still persists. The morals, ethics, and values—the ways of life—have changed, but the people remain. In fact, industrious individuals in most of these lands are still able to achieve wealth and happiness. Even in prison-states like Russia there exists an elite of clever people who manage to live in some degree of luxury. History seems to tell us, then, that the resourcefulness of human beings is virtually boundless. Those blessed with intelligence, marketable skills, imagination, ambition, and/or a penchant for hard work usually do well under any circumstances.

That is not to suggest, however, that you won't be affected by the collapse. You know better than that, because you have already seen your life increasingly affected by it in recent years. The important thing, then, is to put it in proper perspective. Look at it this way: *Everything* in life affects you in one way or another, and a great many things are beyond your control. But that's no cause for panic. Regardless of the nature of any negative circumstance, the best approach is to take rational steps to counteract it. The idea is to maximize the potential of any situation, no matter how unpleasant it may be.

I like the way Viktor Frankl put it in his marvelous book, *Man's Search for Meaning*. It is hard to imagine a situation more dehumanizing or hopeless than being imprisoned in a Nazi concentration camp, as was Frankl for several years. Yet he states that, even while living under those brutal conditions, he realized that "everything can be taken from a man but one thing: the last of the human freedoms—to choose one's attitude in any given set of circumstances, to choose one's own way."

You have it within your power to choose your own way during the continuing collapse of Western Civilization. You have it within your power to make your life prosperous. In the final analysis, it *is* within your control to achieve happiness and success.

A friend of mine, a former top cabinet member in a previous White House administration, recently told me in confidence that he is now 100% sure that the United States is going to experience a "total economic collapse"—that it is now impossible to avoid. Yet he is out wheeling and dealing all over the world, building a tremendous personal fortune.

When I asked him how he can work so hard to increase his wealth, knowing that an economic collapse is inevitable, he said, "I know I'll get caught in the final toppling of the economy, just like everyone else. But I'm gambling that, on a worst-case basis, I might lose only 75% of my wealth through confiscation and ruined investments. The remaining 25%, though, could allow me to live in relative luxury compared to most people. The average American has absolutely no understanding of what is happening, so, of course, he is making no preparations at all." I totally agree.

Why *not* build for the future? Striking out swinging is one thing, but taking a called third strike and going down with the bat on your shoulder is tantamount to default.

During perilous times, one tends to become philosophical about the world, the universe, and man's purpose in life. Since history emphatically demonstrates that very little changes with regard to human nature and the interaction among human beings, it makes one wonder about man's mission—or if he has one. The more I reflect on this question, the more convinced I am that man's fundamental purpose is to achieve; in other words, the striving toward goals is an end in itself.

Viktor Frankl believes that "what man actually needs is not a tensionless state but rather the striving and struggling for some goal worthy of him." After all, if man were to succeed in ridding the world of all disease, poverty, pestilence, famine, and war, what then would be the purpose of his existence? Viewed in that light, it would seem that striving itself—the constant working toward goals—is man's real purpose.

If striving is the essence of a man's life, then it stands to reason that either he continually moves forward or he dies. Thus those who wish their lives away in anticipation of the achievement of some long-awaited goal only cheat themselves. Instead, they should be enjoying every minute of the struggle along the way. They should be concentrating on the joy associated with the day-to-day striving. The future, for many people, is embodied in the shadowy allure of some undefinable promised land down the road. But promised lands are hard to come by. Better to concentrate on enjoying the present.

If you believe that the essence of life is to achieve, and that it is within your power to choose your own way in any set of circumstances, then you already possess the necessary mind-set to achieve happiness during the collapse of Western Civilization. Your starting point is to realistically analyze (meaning to steer clear of government and media distortions) the likely conditions under which you will be striving toward happiness and success. Throughout this book I have tried to assist you in making that analysis.

Next, ask yourself three very important questions:

1. What do I want out of life?
2. What will it cost me (in time, energy, pain, and sacrifice)?
3. Am I willing to pay the necessary price?

Think deeply about the ramifications of these questions before attempting to answer them, as the answers (and your subsequent actions) will determine the outcome of the only life you have. If the questions are not answered honestly, then, of course, the whole exercise is futile.

The objective of the remainder of this book is to help you to answer these questions. I will be describing some of the traits and actions that I believe are necessary to the achievement of happiness and financial success, not just in the environment in which we now live, but in the sort of environment I envision for the future. I want to make you aware of what the costs are likely to be, so you will be able to make a rational determination of your ability and willingness to pay them.

Before moving on, one piece of good news. One of the results of the anything-goes morality that now pervades every level of our society is that people have been encouraged to be lazy, ignorant, and incompetent. This is a plus for you, because it means that you will have relatively little competition if you choose to live in the real world and abide by the unyielding laws of nature. In particular, the laziness, ignorance, and incompetence that is inherent in governments will open up specific opportunities that would not otherwise be available to you.

The premise of this book is therefore simple: The most certain road to success is to do the opposite of that which causes failure. The actions of Western governments have failed. The anything-goes morality has failed. The institutions of Western Civilization are rapidly failing, and all but a small fraction of the population of the Western world is failing along with them.

Solution? Try to do the exact *opposite* of that which has caused these failures. If you can accomplish this, you should indeed find happiness during the collapse of Western Civilization.

SECTION
II

STANDING
RIGHT SIDE
UP
AGAIN

CHAPTER IV

The World According to You

Thomas Paine believed that "the most formidable weapon against errors of every kind is reason." Lacking the ability to reason, a person will perceive the world incorrectly. And the person who perceives the world incorrectly will always be a stranger to happiness and success.

The reason for this is obvious. If your insights are inaccurate, you're bound to make wrong decisions, and I have never yet known a happy or successful person who consistently made wrong decisions. By *perception* or *insight,* I am referring to the ability to interpret correctly the events that surround you—the ability to mentally grasp the difference between the real and the unreal; between what is fact and what is myth; between what works and what doesn't work. I am speaking of perception as the foundation of *your* life.

ACTIONS HAVE CONSEQUENCES

The single most important perception in your life is your broad view of the way the world works. Nature (in an earthly, as opposed to a universal, sense) does not operate in a random fashion. The world runs on a set of unshakable, inviolable principles. It makes no exceptions to these rules, although it sometimes tricks the unwary into believing the contrary. Worse, Nature herself doles out the punishments—often severe—for violations of its rules. Whether one's intentions are good or evil, Nature insists that its rules be adhered to.

The most basic principle of nature—the rule that gives us the clearest insight into how the world works—is: *actions have consequences.* Unfortunately, we all, at times, try to delude ourselves into believing that this principle will not apply to us. In my younger, more naive days, I was often guilty of such delusions, and I still have the scars to prove it.

I can offer no advice that will unconditionally guarantee an individual's happiness or success, but there is definitely one firm guideline for guaranteeing *failure.* It is contained in the *Actions-Have-Consequences Theory,* which states: Refusing to believe that actions have consequences, and acting accordingly, is a victimless crime, punishable by failure. The only way Nature will grant a person a stay of execution is if he repents and forevermore pays homage to this immovable principle.

If you were to analyze the problems of the average individual, you would often find that underlying these problems is a lack of respect for Nature's actions-have-consequences principle. When I refer to *actions,* I am referring to *all* actions (including inaction, which is, in effect, a form of action by default), be they good or bad. Likewise, when I refer to *consequences,* I am referring to *all* consequences, be they good or bad.

If I push you (an action), something *must* happen; i.e., there must be a consequence. Either you will fall down, or you will stumble, or, at the very least, you will feel pressure against your body. In addition, there may be collateral consequences. For example, you may get mad at me, you may walk away from me, or you may push me back. The point is that my action *will* have one or more consequences. I cannot escape that reality. Where I begin to get into trouble is if I delude myself into believing that I can push you without there being any consequences at all.

Suppose I believe that someone has wronged me, and I am so outraged that I decide to sue him. If my actions are dictated only by my anger, or by my adamant belief that I will prevail in court, I am blinding myself to the many other possible consequences of my action. It is important that I correctly perceive all of the potential results of my filing a lawsuit, such as the time, money, and mental anguish involved, not to mention the disgust and frustration of having to witness a bunch of shamelessly unprepared attorneys fake their way through years of litigation, while at the same time doing their best to prolong it. If I do not recognize, in advance, all of the possible consequences, I may well live to regret the filing of the suit—even if I "win."

A more complex example would be the economy. Any individual who today acts on the blind belief that soon everything will be just fine with the economy, guarantees himself disastrous consequences. If he willfully ignores the decades of profligate government spending, inflation of the currency, artificial increases in union wages, ballooning of the national debt, and endless other dishonest and irresponsible actions, he is ensuring that he will be sheared along with the rest of the masses.

The failure of such an individual to acknowledge that all actions have consequences, including the actions of others, will almost certainly lead him into the false-prosperity trap. Because we have been living under the umbrella of false prosperity for so long, it is quite easy for one to falsely perceive one's *true* financial condition. Inflation and government handouts have deluded most people into believing that they are far better off financially than they really are. They *want* to believe that the laws of nature can be reversed; they *want* to believe that two plus two equals five; they *want* to believe that their neighbors will continue to work hard to support them, even though these same neighbors are given less and less incentive to produce. Such fantasies, coupled with the ease of access to installment-credit loans, second and third mortgages, and credit cards (all of which are really indirect methods of increasing the money supply), make it easy for the unwary individual to maintain a grossly inaccurate perception of his financial condition.

As a result, most people, particularly in the United States, are now living well beyond their means. Although this kind of self-deception has always been imprudent, in today's worsening economic climate it spells certain doom. While it is a popular myth that a person should become a debtor during a period of hyperinflation, those who base their actions on this belief are in for some unpleasant surprises as the final scenes of the coming runaway-inflation scenario unfold.*

What such people neglect to plug into their formula is the uncertainty of their future income. In the latter stages of the coming runaway inflation, when a frantic government is shelling out trillions of paper dollars to nonproducers, *you* may not be in a position to get in on the heist. In fact, depending upon the particular skills you possess, there could very possibly be no demand at all for your services during a hyperinflationary stampede.

I envision millions of people in just such a predicament in the years ahead. I picture them staring at their blank television screens (their electricity will have been turned off), while contemplating the worst of all worlds: the prices of the necessities of life have been inflated out of sight; their second- and third-mortgage balloon payments have come due; collection agencies are knocking at their doors, demanding payment on their overdue installment-credit loans; their credit cards have been voided; and their income has been reduced to zero!

Thanks, but no thanks. If I have no choice but to continue to live through this collapse, I can at least choose to sleep at night.

It is crucial to your well-being that you be able to perceive the true consequences of your actions, as well as all other actions that have the capability of affecting your life. In these perilous times, the Actions-Have-Consequences Theory should be first and foremost in your mind. I promise you that there are no exceptions to it, and deluding yourself to the contrary can lead only to disaster.

---

*I do not agree with the currently popular deflationary forecast. While it is conceivable that we could experience a temporary period of deflation, I believe that, in the end, runaway inflation is unavoidable.

THE CRUX OF THE ISSUE

The ability to quickly perceive the crux of every situation, and to act accordingly, is a quality I've come to greatly admire. By perceiving the *crux of the situation,* I mean settling on the issue or issues that need to be decided in order to produce a positive outcome; addressing the fact or facts that can determine success or failure; concentrating on the problem or problems that need to be resolved in order to achieve your major objective.

The average person spends far too much time on irrelevant issues. It is a natural way of life, a predictable offshoot of growing up in a welfare state whose leaders consistently sidestep the crux of most important issues. We are used to hearing the media come up with answers that don't work, because they continually ask the wrong questions. In such an environment, getting at the heart of the matter is not an easy task.

Consequently, when the would-be entrepreneur tries to persuade an investor to back his ideas, and is himself unable to perceive the crux of the issue, he more often than not makes the mistake of dwelling on peripheral considerations that have little or no bearing on the outcome. During a recent discussion of this phenomenon with my friend, Black Bart, he told me that he had developed a way to penetrate the familiar shroud of idea men who make presentations to him.

Black Bart explained that, after giving his visitor a few minutes to state his case, he looks him in the eye and says: "Let's assume that I give you exactly what you want, and that everything goes exactly as you want it to. I want to know only two things: What will you get out of it and what will I get out of it? *The rest doesn't matter."*

Talk about getting straight to the point, this was vintage Black Bart. He went on to say that he was repeatedly amazed, not only that so few people actually work out the specific answers to these questions in advance, but that so few even think about them. They are usually either too dazzled by the more glamorous aspects of the deal—the "sizzle"—or else sidetracked by irrelevant details.

As I sat there frantically taking notes on the back of my tie, I asked Black Bart to elaborate on his contention that "the rest doesn't matter." He revealed that, in all the years he spent in the building business (where he made his original fortune), he never learned how to read a blueprint, he never learned how to dig a foundation, he never even learned how to drive a nail. And now, today, after earning enough money in the petroleum business to buy Poland and Hungary and give back Uganda in change, Black Bart says that he still doesn't know how to drill a gas well. His view is that reading blueprints and drilling gas wells are *hired skills.* So that's exactly what he does—hires them. That frees him to spend *his* time on the issues that ultimately decide the success or failure of any given project.

You may not be in a position to hire all the skills you would like to farm out, but that's not the point. Black Bart was merely trying to emphasize the importance of learning to recognize what's crucial to money-making results and what isn't. No matter on what level you're playing the game at any given time, the important thing is to resist the temptation to be diverted by issues that are not critical to bringing about a "payoff."

Another friend of mine, Trader Bill, has demonstrated an uncanny flair for getting to the crux of the matter without delay. After going broke in 1970, he got up off the canvas, took the mandatory eight count, and plunged back in—with no capital, no credit, and a bankruptcy on his record. In a period of approximately ten years, he managed to develop no less than twenty-three office buildings. Most of the buildings are located in the San Francisco and Houston areas, the majority ranging in size from 100,000 to 225,000 square feet.

How is it possible for a man to complete so many major projects in such a short period of time? Obviously, he could never have accomplished so much so quickly if he were bogged down in details. From observing his method of operation, I believe that his number-one asset is his ability to perceive the difference between material and peripheral considerations. He doesn't try to be a brick or concrete expert, an engineer, or an architect. He doesn't even claim to be a contractor. It's interesting to note that, even though he is referred to as the "builder" of each building, he has no hand in the actual construction. Instead, he hires a general contractor, who in turn subcontracts out the various aspects of the job. Few people realize that most major "builders" do not actually do construction. They view it as a hired skill and spend their time on the creative issues that ultimately determine profit or loss.

To the textbook communist, Trader Bill is the archetypical capitalist who "produces nothing." It is terribly hard for the egalitarian mind to comprehend what it is that Trader does. But, in reality, his job—putting the deal together—is the most important of all. He focuses only on the big issues—selecting the right land, obtaining the financing, hiring the best general contractor—factors that are *crucial* to the success or failure of the project.

Does this sound too easy? No pain? Quite the contrary. What Trader Bill does is excruciatingly painful. Those who perform the hired skills have only to do the job that is laid out for them. The general contractor, for example, does only what he is paid to do—build the building on the site where he is told to build it. He doesn't need to worry about putting the project together; he simply performs a function. Were it not for the big-picture efforts of men like Trader Bill, general contractors would have nothing to build.

Perhaps the true essence of getting to the crux of the matter was best expressed by the Red Baron, a friend of mine who lives in Las Vegas. Red, now in his mid-seventies, suffered a stroke a few years back, but is still playing the game with zest. He never misses a day at the office and rarely, if ever, misses a trick. He finds time to fly down to New Zealand now and then, on his seventeen-passenger Gulfstream jet, to visit his 33,000-acre sheep ranch; or hop over to South Carolina to check on his crab-packing plant; or go to Switzerland to see how his bank is doing (by "his" bank, I mean just that—*his* bank). His nine-figure net worth is *not* composed of inflated real-estate values, overstated stocks, or privately owned companies with little marketability. It is made up of *hard assets,* with no liabilities to speak of. So when the Red Baron talks, The Tortoise listens—*closely.*

One day, during one of our fireside chats, the Red Baron said to me: "Do you know all there is to making money? You sell your product or service for the highest possible price; you keep your expenses as low as possible; and in between is your profit." You can't make it any simpler than that; profit is *really* the heart of the issue. In the words of Black Bart, the rest simply doesn't matter. Yet most people insist on dwelling on everything *but* the bottom line, and, not surprisingly, most people fail.

The legendary Bernard Baruch summed up the importance of perceiving the crux of the issue like this:

> Mankind has always sought to substitute energy for reason, as if running faster will give one a better sense of direction. Periodically we should stop and ask ourselves if our efforts are focused upon the crux of the problem—the things that must be settled if there is to be a manageable solution—or if we are expending our energies on side issues which cannot yield a decision, no matter what their outcome.

THE LAZY MAN'S WAY TO POVERTY

I am constantly amused—as well as fascinated—by the popular perception of how successful people make money. There is a widely held, vague notion that the "heavy hitters" of the business world sit in their ivory towers by day and leisurely press rows of magical buttons that instantly make their every wish come true. Away from their office thrones, they are envisioned flitting about in their private jets, buying up professional sports franchises like so many toys, and generally leading party-filled lives that are occasionally interrupted by work.

To further distort reality, the media does its best to suggest

*"Down, boy, down. Keep calm and the Red Baron will toss
you a few more morsels of wisdom."*

that such men are brutal and greedy, and, most of all, "insensitive to the needs of others." Always there is the suggestion that these mountain-movers have taken too big a slice of the pie, leaving only a pittance in crumbs for others. No mention is made of the fact that tens of thousands of people owe their jobs to the genius of such men.

Unfortunately (or fortunately, depending on where your head is), my firsthand experience with several financial heavyweights makes it clear that, as is often the case, the myth and the reality are far removed from one another. In every instance, I find there is an urgency about such men, a need to get down in the trenches where they can at least closely monitor the situation, if not actually lead the charge. There is a kind of nervous energy that compels them to move forward and achieve. They rarely sit anywhere for very long, let alone in an ivory tower.

The typical human by-product of an upside-down world thinks only in terms of, "I want to *have*." The self-made man thinks, "I want to *achieve*." The wide disparity between the success and failure of two such individuals clearly reflects the wide disparity in their thinking. The emphasis on "wanting" (which today equates to "getting") is part and parcel of the moral revolution's elevation of desires to rights. This concept has destroyed the minds—and thus the earning capacity—of a majority of citizens in Western nations.

If a person's mind is preoccupied with what he has been told are his "rights," he has no time to think about how wealth is actually created. Instead, he focuses on the rules that protect these so-called rights. Is his employer paying him according to government-imposed wage guidelines? Is he getting the number of coffee breaks politicians have said he is entitled to? Are his working conditions in line with bureaucratic mandates?

Such questions are the major concerns of most workers. No one has time to actually accomplish anything; everyone is too busy checking out his "rights." "Overtime" work is a good example. Workers have been assured by the government that they are "entitled" to time-and-a-half pay. Of course, no one ever asks why the employer isn't entitled to time-and-a-half *work*. (Oh, for the days of Ebenezer Scrooge, when getting Christmas Eve off was cause for Bob Cratchit to celebrate.)

In today's mob-rule atmosphere it is only natural for a worker to think this way. Everywhere he turns—the media, his friends, associates, schools—he is constantly reminded that he has a "right" to make others, through government force, accede to his desires. He hears very little, if anything, about how to motivate an employer, through his own accomplishments, to *voluntarily* pay him the salary to which he aspires.

At the heart of the problem is that most people have absolutely no idea how wealth is created. Wealth is produced through *effort,* both creative and physical. There is certainly no mystery to it, even though our institutions have for years been teaching otherwise. We have been led to believe that wealth somehow just exists, in a limitless supply and without any effort involved to produce it, and that it therefore can be handed out to nonproducers indefinitely.

It is this misconception about the creation of wealth that has led not only to the fiscal bankruptcy of the Western world, but to the financial failure of most individuals as well. It is this underlying belief—that men can increase their financial well-being without work—that has also led them to have false perceptions of how "big money" is made.

People in today's upside-down world are eager to believe any bromide about making money that does not involve sacrifice—no hard work, no self-discipline, no patience, no pain. Thus the perpetuation of a variety of myths about the making of quick and easy fortunes. For example, the masses like to believe that a person can dabble in a number of occupations or projects at the same time, cavalierly raking in chips along the way. Bernard Baruch expressed his feelings about this naiveté clearly when he stated: "[A] common illusion some people have is that they can do anything—buy and sell stocks, dabble in real estate, run a business, engage in politics—all at once. My own experience is that few men can do more than one thing at a time—and do it well."

Don't be taken in by guys who drive big Cadillacs, smoke expensive cigars, and mumble about "selling a little real estate," "placing a little insurance now and then," "putting together a consortium of investors here and there," and "dabbling in a few businesses." That simply isn't the way it works in the real world. The big boys don't dabble; they excel at singleness of purpose and bust their buns trying to achieve that purpose.

Another convenient substitute for the reality that hard work is an inescapable ingredient of success is the idea that success is the result of genius. In a sense, this is more an excuse for failure than a hope for success, and it mixes well with the smog of envy that hangs heavy over our collectivist atmosphere.

Take, for example, Indian-born Sirjang Lal "Jugi" Tandon, founder and head of Tandon Corporation. After just six years in business (the company manufactures disc drives for small computers), Tandon's sales are projected at $130 million. The company is debt free and enjoys a cash position of some $50 million.

To most people, it would appear that Mr. Tandon was simply an electronics genius who happened to come along at the right time and had the opportunity to apply his particular expertise to a made-to-order situation. But the reality is quite different. What caught my eye in a recent article about Mr. Tandon, who had taken many risks and slowly saved $7,000 to get started, was his own description of the early days of his company when *he himself cleaned the bathrooms and swept the floors.*

The average blue-collar worker, however, considers such chores beneath him—which is why he remains a blue-collar worker. It is much more comfortable to exclude ourselves from the competition by believing that a man of Mr. Tandon's success made it to the top simply because of his superior intellect. Claude Hopkins, the legendary turn-of-the-century advertising magnate, put the matter in proper perspective when he noted that "genius is the art of taking pains." The reality is that genius doesn't cause success; it is success that causes one to be called a genius.

More than anything, my own experience as an author has helped me to see just how erroneous is the average person's per-

"Christmas Eve off, eh? I want my time-and-a-half overtime work, and I want it now."

ception of what it takes to make money. Over the years, I have been on the receiving end of more than just a few comments to the effect that, "It must be nice not to have to work for a living— just knock out a book every couple of years and live the good life in between."

There's no question in my mind that most of the people who have uttered statements like this have really believed what they were saying, even though their tone has usually been somewhat tongue-in-cheek. Normally, my response has been nonverbal; a patronizing smile is all that is warranted. I figure there's no sense trying to explain something to a person who has absolutely no concept of what it takes to do a job that is totally foreign to him.

What does it *really* take to write a book? To paraphrase Red Smith, the late and legendary sports columnist, writing is easy— all you do is sit down to a typewriter every day, cut open a vein, and bleed a little.

Having been there many times, I believe that even Mr. Smith's description of what it takes to write a book is a bit rose-colored. Throughout my life, I have been involved in a wide variety of occupations and business ventures, from traveling salesman to real estate entrepreneur, from construction worker to president of a public company. Many a time I have worked around the clock preparing a presentation, then taken the "red-eye special" coast to coast in a frantic effort to put a deal together. Often I was so tired that I started to doubt that any reward, no matter how great, could be worth it. Yet none of these experiences—no matter how physically debilitating, no matter how mentally exhausting, no matter how uncomfortable—even begins to approach the pains and sacrifice associated with writing a (good) book.

I inserted the word *good* in parentheses because of what my comedy-writer friend, Chubby Chuckle, once told me. In response to my asking him if writing jokes is hard, he replied: "No, it isn't hard at all to write a joke. But to write a *good* joke is torture!"

Arthur Hailey let the public in on the painful truth about

what it takes to be a good writer when he confessed: "I set a quota of six hundred words a day. I actually count the words, as pedantic as that sounds. I may go over them 10 or 20 times before I'm happy." Imagine painstakingly reworking each sentence of a book as many as twenty times! Just the thought of such a task is enough to make one's brain explode.

Does that mean that I'd rather be, say, a carpenter than a writer if I could make just as much money? You bet it does! It wouldn't even be a close decision. I find carpentry relaxing and therapeutic. I find the most menial tasks to be soothing. But writing a book is like having the Ayatollah tease your brain with an electric cattle prod.

Because I'm so aware of the irreconcilable breach between the misperception and the reality of what it takes to write a book, I never kid myself about someone else's success in another field. When I look at another man's accomplishments, they may appear easy from where I'm sitting, but I know better. I just assume that his degree of financial success is directly proportionate to the amount of pain he has endured.

Another popular myth that has been nurtured in our no-pain-at-any-cost environment is that success should be *immediate*. Politicians help to nurture this fantasy, because to them there is no long term; the next election is always just around the corner. That's why a politician's every sales pitch promises immediate gratification. After fifty years of doling out instant well-being to voters, is it any wonder that they cling to the notion of instant success? The thought of pain must be avoided at all costs.

Thus stories of meteoric rises to success abound. Take, for example, my friend High Noon Harry, who started an oil company from scratch about eight years ago. In that brief span, he built his firm from ground zero to a $5-billion-dollar-a-year petroleum giant—*privately owned*. So astonishing an ascent to such rarified financial heights is awesome, to be sure. Unfortunately, however, such an example encourages many people to cling to the hope that "it" could "happen" to them, too. The problem is that they have absolutely no idea what "it" is. And they do not understand that nothing "happened" to High Noon Harry. It was quite the other way around: He *made* things happen.

To begin with, it's an illusion to think that High Noon built his company in a mere eight years, even though, technically, that's how long he's been in business for himself. What none of the stories about him explains, however, is that he first spent twenty-five years laying the groundwork for success while in the employ of others. He spent thirteen years at Tenneco, Inc., learning the oil business from the ground up, at the knee of the legendary Gardiner Symonds. He later joined Occidental Petroleum, as president of a Canadian subsidiary, where he continued his "apprenticeship" for another five years under the tutelage of Armand Hammer.

When High Noon Harry finally decided that he had paid his dues and had acquired sufficient knowledge of the oil business, he left the security of Occidental Petroleum to start his own company. His initial investment was the grand sum of $1,000. But the most important investment he made in his new company was the thousands of hours he had spent traveling the world for his employers during the previous twenty-five years, the sweat and energy invested on their behalf, and the many years of laborious study of the petroleum business.

His good name throughout the industry paid dividends shortly after his company came into existence. At that time a major oil company wanted to accumulate a considerable amount of #2 heating oil, but did not want to go into the open market for fear that their buying would rapidly push up its price. Instead, they approached High Noon Harry, along with one other expert trader, and asked him to "front" for them in the market. High Noon eventually bought some 690,000 barrels of #2 heating oil for this oil company, which, after only a few months in business, yielded him a profit of $200,000.

Then, within a year, he made his first million-dollar deal. He had gotten wind of an oil sale that was to be made by a foreign-government-owned oil company, and wasted no time jetting to South America and making a bid. Because of High Noon Harry's wide contacts and knowledge of the industry, he was able to *pre-sell* the oil to another company at a $1-million profit to himself. Based on the government's commitment to sell the oil and the commitment of the other company to buy it, he was then able to obtain bank letters of credit sufficient to make the necessary purchase.

From that auspicious beginning, his company jumped to $1 billion in sales in 1975, and in each succeeding year the graph continued sharply upward. But all the public sees is the glamor of a man who built a giant corporation "overnight." What they don't see—and, in fact, don't want to see—are the twenty-five years of time, energy, sacrifice, and study that positioned High Noon Harry to go for the big chips—not to mention the time, energy, sacrifice, and risks he has since invested in his own business. The truth is that one can make a justifiable argument that High Noon's company was twenty-five-years old the day it began.

I would not want you to infer from this discussion that all it takes to succeed is hard work. That is absolutely untrue. What I am saying is that hard work is one of the mandatory components of the success equation. Everyone who succeeds has it in his formula; but if it's the *only* thing you rely on, you will *not* succeed.

A majority of people, not wanting to face the reality that sacrifice goes hand in hand with success, are destined always to perceive successful individuals as being either very lucky or very smart. In their minds, the mysterious inhabitants of that faraway kingdom vaguely referred to as "the big time" were merely smiled upon, inexplicably, by good fortune.

Such a perception is essential to the way of life of the average person. First, it justifies his envy. Second, it allows him to hold out hope that he, too, may someday get "lucky" and make a fortune. If you'd like to play footsie with failure, all you need do is embrace this pipe-dream perception of what it takes to make money. Regardless of the wishes of the Western world's collectivist planners, Nature stubbornly refuses to reward people just for being alive.

REAL PEOPLE

Since we live in a division-of-labor world, we have no choice but to work with, and rely upon, other human beings. Maintaining a good track record in correctly judging people is therefore basic to success, both financial and social.

People, on the whole, are either *as* they seem, *less* than they seem, or *more* than they seem. Your job is to determine which. It's a tricky business, as evidenced by Black Bart's assertion that "your ears are to hear only what your eyes miss." In other words, pay attention to what people *do,* not just what they say. Your people perceptions are an integral part of your everyday life, so you can expect them to yield significant consequences.

Following are a few examples of the types of obstacles that can make it very difficult to judge whether a person is as, less, or more than he seems.

Self-Advertising

In a society where false prosperity is a cherished way of life, and where people believe they should be rewarded just for breathing, it is quite natural that individuals should have an inflated perception of their own worth. Most people today can't even *spell* competent, let alone *be* competent. Thus, there are millions of applicants visiting personnel offices every year who have delusions of competency. Consequently, to avoid being financially drowned in a sea of delusions, you must learn to perceive the abilities of others—*without regard to their own perceptions of themselves.*

For the ever-vigilant, the warning signals can eventually be detected. One such giveaway is the individual who makes too forceful a case for himself. This often happens during job interviews. From the fallout of the collapse of our societal structure, a whole cult of people have grown up who, lacking skill, competence, and/or ambition, have become amazingly adept at fooling interviewers.

The objective today is not to become competent at a *job;* it is to become competent at being *interviewed.* This is costly for employers, because it means that more often than ever they are hiring people whose job performances turn out to be quite different from their interview performances. I used to think I was quite good at judging prospects during interviews, but I simply have not been able to keep pace with the new-morality interview skills.

One recent example involved my search for a high-quality "executive secretary." After interviewing many prospects, one candidate impressed me by coming right out in the interview and telling me that she was "the best." Of course, because she was the best, she wanted a starting salary that was far in excess of any that I had previously paid. I bit.

Ignorantly, I based *my* perception of her on *her* perception of *herself.* My reasoning was that no one would have the nerve to make such a bold statement if she could not back it up. I countered with an offer that was still higher than any executive-secretary salary I had previously paid, but she stood firm. She pointed out that the amount she was asking was what she had already been earning at her previous job, and that she could not bring herself to come down to my figure since she was sure that she could get her asking price in the "open market."

I finally suggested that we compromise at a figure only slightly below her request, and that after she learned our systems and office procedures and had had the opportunity to clearly demonstrate her abilities to us, we would then talk about raising her salary to the figure she was requesting. With a great deal of reluctance, she finally agreed to go along with my proposal.

The result? After a couple of weeks, I noticed a few things that Ms. Best was doing wrong, but I wasn't too concerned about them, because I had the comfort of knowing that she was "the best." After all, she had told me so—which was the sole basis for my perception of her! While complimenting her on her "progress," I also casually suggested that there were a "few areas" where she might want to sharpen up a bit—such as trying not to make so many assumptions (which always led to making mistakes), being more alert when listening to dictation (so as to make fewer of *those* mistakes), and cutting down on her social calls during business hours (*always* a mistake).

By the third month, I was ready to concede that perhaps Ms. Best was not "the best" after all. To those in the office who were thinking more in terms of setting the back of her hair on fire, I said, "Look, maybe she isn't quite as good as I thought, but she *is* good. She just seems to have mental lapses now and then."

By the end of the fourth month, I was weakening: "All right, I admit she makes a lot of mistakes. I admit she sometimes forgets to write up phone messages. I admit she has a habit of making costly assumptions. But she *is* mechanically proficient."

By the fifth month, it was *I* who was considering putting a torch to her hair. The final corner was turned one day when I called her into my office to point out another mistake she had made. The mistake had resulted in some costly repercussions, and I was hoping to forestall a repetition of the unhappy event in the future. Her first reaction was to tell me that it was I who was mistaken, that my recollection of my own instructions was incorrect. After I strongly suggested that my instructions had, in fact, been as I had stated, Ms. Best broke into tears and ran out of my office. It certainly was a touching sight—extraordinarily appropriate business behavior for an executive secretary.

Subsequently, she reviewed her own transcription notes and found, to her chagrin, that she had been wrong. Did that prompt her to offer a brief and immediate apology? Hardly. Instead, she typed up a two-page explanation of the situation, on company time, in which she admitted her mistake, but zeroed in on the fact that my "handling of the situation begged for defensive action" on her part.

At that point, I realized that I was faced with an important decision. Either I had to go into the professional babysitting business full time or admit to the rest of the office that I had made a grave mistake. I decided on the latter. Not only was Ms. Best guilty of all the aforementioned sins, but, notwithstanding my previous insistences to the contrary, she was not even mechanically proficient.

Alas, the truth had to be faced. Actions have consequences. My perception had been based on Ms. Best's self-advertising—

and we had both been way off the mark. If she was "the best," then I was Joe Montana. She was *not* "the best"; she was *not* good; she was *not* average; she was *not* bad. She was, in point of fact, the *worst*—a living, breathing, full-fledged incompetent, fit only for employment by a government agency.

People with inflated self-perceptions are really guilty of self-delusion; i.e., they base their actions on who and what they would like to be, rather than who and what they really are. In the long run, their faulty self-perception is always costly to them, usually because it results in their being unemployed, or, if in business for themselves, stands in the way of their making profits (deal making is almost impossible if a person has delusions about what he brings to the deal).

Don't be impressed by anyone who claims to be "the best." Let him *prove* it. One footnote: Be careful about harboring grandiose perceptions of *yourself* that cannot be backed by accomplishments.

Denying Your Instincts

Then there are those daring souls who, within a short time of managing to bluff their way through the job interview, unwisely press their luck by making new demands. This happened with another young lady whom I had hired on the misguided notion that, because her attitude was good, she could gradually decrease her ineptitude. Because of my sweet, benevolent nature, I steadfastly clung to this foundationless hope, keeping her on long after it had become obvious that she would never learn how to set the tabs on her typewriter, let alone press the necessary keys. She wanted to please so badly that I just couldn't bring myself to let her go. I, too, had delusions. I thought my name was Friar Tortoise and that I was running a nonprofit organization.

You probably assume that, given the circumstances, this young woman just came right out and admitted that she couldn't cut it and, in a show of integrity, volunteered to take a pay cut in exchange for being allowed to stay on in some lesser capacity.

"Glad to meet you, Ms. Best. Just call me Joe."

Sure she did. On the contrary, she requested a hearing one day, whereupon she made two requests. First, she wanted to move up to something *more challenging* than the work that had already proved to be over her head. Second, she wanted a *raise*.

I had no choice but to fall back on the Vince Lombardi Policy. At the peak of Lombardi's career at Green Bay, the player-agent phenomenon was just beginning to take hold. He was from the old school and didn't quite understand an athlete's being represented by a runny-nosed kid in a three-piece suit, sporting Gucci loafers and argyle socks. The first time that a player came in to tell Lombardi that his agent would be calling Lombardi to negotiate his contract, the master supposedly replied, "Tell him not to bother. You've just been traded to Philadelphia."

My response was Lombardian to the core. Without hesitation, I traded this hallucinating young lady to New Orleans for a delivery boy, a used IBM Selectric typewriter, and a box of felt-tipped pens. Other than that, all it took was a smile, a severance check, and a good-luck wish, and the problem was solved.

Another time that denying my instincts caused me undue problems was when I hired an overbearing, hard-sell type by the name of Ollie Oink. Ollie had "flake" written across his forehead the first time he walked through my door, and I must admit that I clearly read the word. But, because he talked (boy, did he ever talk) so convincingly, I *wanted* to believe that he was creditable.

About a year after hiring Ollie, I became involved in putting together some backing to buy controlling interest in a New York Stock Exchange company that had a strong liquid-asset position. The firm was based in Detroit, while the investor I had been talking to about backing me in the takeover bid lived in New York. After investing a considerable amount of time and money in the deal, which included several trips to New York, Murphy's Law began to take effect.

To avoid spreading myself too thin, I decided to turn the project over to Ollie Oink. At the time, I believed (or wanted to believe) that he was the right person for the job, because he had demonstrated such great enthusiasm for every task to which he

"You'll just love New Orleans in the summer, and I'm sure you'll find the work much more challenging there."

had previously been assigned. His fervor, however, went beyond just plain enthusiasm; he was aggressive to the point of bordering on obnoxious. His constant rhetoric about what steps needed to be taken for "the good of the company" were impressive, but his *actions* raised many an eyebrow among people both in and out of the office.

At that stage of my career, my perception was not sufficiently refined to understand that "what a person *is* speaks so loudly that I can hardly hear his words." I had received a number of complaints about Ollie Oink, complaints that clearly challenged his integrity. On several occasions, both friends and business associates had cautioned me to "watch out for that guy." In fact, before I hired him, an acquaintance had warned me that he was the most avaricious person he had ever known.

But I opted to deny both my own intuition and the warnings of others. A couple of weeks and several trips to New York later, Ollie Oink asked to speak to me in private. Settling into a chair opposite my desk and lighting up a cigarette, he proceeded to tell me, in a somewhat trembling voice that belied his outward boldness, that he had worked out the backing of the New York investor—not for me, but for himself!

He claimed that he had convinced the investor that he was more capable than I of putting together the deal to gain control of the listed company, and that the investor had agreed to back him rather than me. Sustaining himself with the salary I had been paying him, plus the use of my offices, telephones, and travel subsidies, Ollie Oink had for weeks not only been moonlighting, but moonlighting on *my deal.*

The story has a happy ending, of sorts, in that he did not, in fact, succeed in acquiring the company. For that matter, he didn't even come close. When I later talked to the New York investor, whose reputation was impeccable, he told me that Ollie Oink had been dreaming—that he had never given him any encouragement whatsoever about backing him in the deal. (Fantasizing about the status of a deal is, by the way, one of the surest signs of a loser, but that's a different matter altogether.)

The important point is that I had totally ignored my intuition, which had told me that this fellow's motives were highly suspect. I credited him with good intentions solely because I *wanted* his intentions to be good. But one's desires regarding someone else's motives are irrelevant; his *actual* motives are what count. Make sure that you're able to perceive the difference between the two.

Ollie Oink may have faded into oblivion in the fields of flaky promoters, but I certainly gained a lot from the experience. I realized that unless I planned to live in a cave in the Andes, I had better start respecting my own intuition. As the collapse of Western Civilization worsens, it will become ever more important for you to discipline yourself to listen to your instincts.

Premature Evaluations

Many years ago I was involved in a summit with several officers of a large New York corporation. I and an associate, along with three members of the New York company, engaged in some preliminary chatting while awaiting the arrival of another of their staff. When I asked whom we were waiting for, one of the company's negotiating-team members said, half-jokingly, "our shark."

When the "shark"—Darby Dan—finally made his appearance, I immediately perceived trouble. Behind his scowl I detected an ill-omened, play-it-by-the-book corporate attitude that held the promise of being a blockade to the negotiations. As he took his seat, I leaned over to my associate and whispered, "Mark my words, he's the deal-killer." Because of this preconceived image of Darby Dan, every time he opened his mouth I felt obliged to counter with a subtle but contrary suggestion. Luckily for me, this didn't seem to alienate him, and we somehow managed to get through that meeting and ultimately conclude an agreement.

Subsequently, the nature of my dealings with this company resulted in my having almost daily communication with Darby

Dan, and, after a few months of working with him, I became perplexed. It wasn't just that we managed to close the original deal, but Darby always seemed to have a way of solving virtually every problem that arose thereafter.

It finally became apparent that not only was he not a deal-killer, but, on the contrary (and to my embarrassment), he was an insatiable, though prudent, deal-*maker.* I don't think I have ever worked with anyone who has had a propensity for solving problems as quickly as he, or who was more enthusiastic about getting deals closed without any undue fuss.

It's amazing how an off-the-cuff prior comment can influence one's impression of a person. And if the person innocently plays into the mistaken impression or prior comment when you meet him, he's as good as indicted. But behavioral clues, while important, constitute only circumstantial evidence, as was the case with Darby Dan. The decision to convict or acquit should be made only after one amasses more solid evidence—*the evidence of actions taken.*

Hearsay

Playful, off-the-cuff remarks are one thing, but elaborate, volunteered second- and third-hand story-telling is quite another. Goebbel's Law—"the louder the abuse, the bigger the lie"—is oft-practiced. Because of the somewhat radical abuse heaped on The Tortoise by his friends in the media over the years, who have succeeded brilliantly in creating a mythical "Ringer image," I am particularly reluctant to judge people on hearsay.

The media thrive on big-bad-wolf stories. It is understandable, then, why the title of my first book, *Winning Through Intimidation*, was just too irresistible for them to pass up. The fact that many of these so-called critics admitted to never having read the book was irrelevant to them—and their readers. By their account, *Winning Through Intimidation* was a guide on how to get ahead by intimidating others. In point of fact (and as everyone who has read the book knows), it was primarily a book on how to *defend oneself against intimidating people* (such as those in the media).

As a result of this unrelenting stream of media nonsense, people who deal with me for the first time are often forearmed with faulty, and sometimes ludicrous, perceptions. What this does is to distort my actions and words in their minds, because they are predisposed to translating my every word and move in light of what they *think* they know about me.

I never cease to be surprised at the way some people insist on interpreting my actions. One such gentleman, a businessman from Atlanta, had occasion to recount to an associate of mine an "intimidating encounter" he had had with me in New Orleans, as follows: "I was given the full Ringer intimidation treatment; you wouldn't have believed it. I go up to his hotel room, and someone lets me in. It's an awesome, palatial suite, and I'm led to a table and asked to sit down. Then Ringer comes marching out in his robe, with a *stopwatch* in his hand. He sits down, puts the stopwatch on the table, and tells me that I have only fifteen minutes. At the end of fifteen minutes, he rises and informs me that the meeting is over. If I hadn't read about him in advance, I would have been bowled over."

Wrong. If he hadn't read about me in advance, I don't think he would have given my actions much thought one way or another. Certainly he would not have interpreted events as he did. The fact of the matter is that when this particular gentleman had called and asked if we could get together to discuss a matter of mutual interest, I was under tremendous time pressure. I therefore wanted him to know, up front, that I could spare only fifteen minutes. If I have a time problem, as a matter of courtesy I always try to let the other person know about it in advance. That way he is unlikely to be offended if, after a previously agreed-upon period of time, we have to terminate our meeting.

When this particular gentleman arrived at my hotel suite, I was scurrying about, trying to get dressed and, at the same time, gathering paperwork for my ensuing meetings. After an associate showed the gentleman into the suite, I quickly threw on a robe and came into the living room. (The suite consisted of two bedrooms—another party of two was with me—and a sitting room. Hardly palatial.) I happen to carry a pocket watch (*not* a stopwatch) instead of wearing a wristwatch, and I am, by nature, very time-conscious. It was therefore quite natural for me to have my watch in hand as I sat down. I apologized profusely for being in a hurry, and, as promised, at the end of fifteen minutes I explained that I had other commitments and had to be moving along.

Until six months later, when this gentleman offered his highly dramatic account of our meeting, I had not given the matter a second thought. I was truly amazed to hear how he had perceived me—and still am. Even so, this is hardly the first time that I have had such an experience, and I have accustomed myself to expect that there will be many more of a similar nature in the future.

As a result of the media's fixation with the "intimidation thing," I find that people often wear mental six-shooters on their hips when negotiating with me. I sometimes feel like putting a sign on my door:

PLEASE CHECK

HANDGUNS

WITH RECEPTIONIST.

THANK YOU.

It is often quite humorous to watch a newcomer on the other side of the negotiating table wasting vast amounts of time and energy concentrating on one-upmanship, not realizing that my only intention is to get the facts out in the open and conclude a deal as quickly and simply as possible. I often have the feeling that the other person thinks that he and I are playing some sort of game, and I'm sometimes tempted to burst his bubble by breaking the news to him that he's playing alone. The irony is that, as a result of such a person's hearsay-based perception of me, he often ends up taking actions that are for the most part self-defeating.

"All right, T.T. Ah'm ready to negotiate."

Whether you're dealing with people or issues, your challenge is to correctly interpret the world in which you live—i.e., to properly perceive the difference between that which is real and that which is unreal. Accurate perception is the first chapter of every true-life story with a happy ending. To make sure that *your* story ends on a happy note during the coming turbulent years, you must continually monitor your powers of perception. If you don't allow your emotions to cloud the reality that actions have consequences, the likelihood is that most of your consequences will be positive.

CHAPTER V

If Your Hands
Are Clean

If sound perception is the foundation for success, honesty is the skeletal structure. By *honesty,* I am speaking of a refusal to lie, steal, cheat, or deceive in any way.

Unfortunately, we live in a world where honesty is, at best, undervalued; at worst, scorned. In the aftermath of the moral revolution, lying, stealing, cheating, and deception are today not only accepted, but encouraged. From a very early age, we are taught to assimilate dishonest premises and to accept them as moral. Bertrand Russell was all too accurate when he noted that "the government distorts the minds of the young and calls it education."

The precepts of the moral revolution are false, and the consequences are now coming home to roost. The belief that wealth can be created without work is a lie; the claim that inflation is caused by the Arab oil cartel or profit-hungry corporations is a lie; the notion that equality and freedom can coexist is a lie; the theory that there is only a fixed amount of wealth on the earth, and that an excess of wealth in the hands of one person therefore impoverishes others, is a lie; and so-called liberalism, in all its forms, including "socialism," "communism," and "Marxism," is a lie.

65

When the moral seams of a society are sewn of lies such as these, as ours now are, it is hardly surprising that the people who make up that society lie, steal, cheat, and deceive almost as a way of life. I do not say that most people today *think* that they lie, steal, cheat, and deceive; they simply *do* lie, steal, cheat, and deceive, regardless of whether or not they are conscious of it. On the contrary, you would be hard pressed to find someone who really *believes* that he is guilty of these actions.

What allows otherwise well-meaning people to delude themselves on the honesty issue is that they have dined too often at the egalitarian table, where dishonest actions are routinely served up in a way that makes them palatable. In time they even taste honest. And they are—in a world turned upside down! Theft is not theft so long as you call it welfare. Fraud is not fraud so long as you call it inflation. Lying is not lying so long as you call it politics.

Come one, come all—jump in and learn to play the game. No action is dishonest if you know how to label it. The world is one big insane asylum, where the caretakers (governments) have gone mad. The inmates (the public), following their cue, are having a ball. Anything—*absolutely anything*—goes! In such an environment, the most dishonest person would be outright indignant if you so much as suggested that his actions are less than scrupulous.

You would be wise not to get caught up in this tempest of immorality. The ship of Western society is tossing about wildly, and its passengers are grasping at everything in sight in a frantic effort to save their hides. So hold on to your senses—and your morals. Instead of yielding to the temptation to follow the crowd, have the self-discipline to do the *opposite* of what the majority of men do and you will be among the few to survive and prosper.

"THE LIE THAT ISN'T A 'REAL' LIE"

When I say that most people lie, steal, cheat, and deceive as a way of life, I mean it quite literally. The average person participates in dishonest actions many, many times each day. This is particularly true of lying. He lies almost reflexively, without even giving it a second thought. Why should he? His mind has been programmed to accept basic falsehoods as truths, so he is no longer capable of distinguishing between the two.

It is, however, critical to your success—in fact, to your very survival—that *you* be able to correctly interpret the actions and statements of others; i.e., that you be able to evaluate whether others are honest or dishonest. Your best-laid plans will surely be destroyed if you allow dishonest people easy access to your life. To help you identify such people, I am going to address some of the more common types of lies, falsehoods that the average Western man no longer sees as "real" lies. Predictably, the evolution of the "lie that isn't a real lie" has paved the way for everyone to seriously defend *his own* lies. (To avoid being repetitious, the emphasis throughout this chapter will be on lying, though you should have no problem extending everything I will be saying to stealing, cheating, and deceiving.)

The Little White Lie

When a businessman instructs his secretary to tell a caller that he's not in, he is *lying;* but he doesn't *think* of it as lying. When someone invites you out socially, and you invent an excuse to avoid going, you are *lying;* but you don't *think* of it as lying. When a parent tells a ticket seller at a movie house that his thirteen-year-old son is only twelve, hoping to pay a lower rate, the parent is *lying;* but he doesn't *think* of it as lying.

In their haste to defend themselves, most people, given examples like these, insist that they involve only "little white lies," and that no one is really harmed by them. My response to that is the *Little-White-Lie Theory:* Little white lies wouldn't cause too many problems of and by themselves, but they tend to lead to big black lies, which cause a *lot* of problems.

Little white lies to help solve select problems lead to harmful lies for much the same reason that the use of majority rule to help select groups of people leads to an anything-goes society: human nature. Once a person gets away with a small and seemingly harmless dishonest act (such as welfare payments to "the poor"), it is human nature to attempt the ruse again and again—on a larger and larger scale.

This is precisely how the little-white-welfare lie escalated into the big-black-welfare lie of today. The use of majority rule to fulfill the scant "needs" of a small number of people at the lowest end of the income spectrum appeared harmless in the beginning, but the probably well-meaning proponents of such action did not take *human nature* into account. The "truly needy," we were led to believe, were a handful of sick, elderly, helpless people living on the edge of starvation. And there really *were* (and are) some sick, elderly, helpless people who were (and are) badly in need of charity. But once this argument was successfully employed to dip into taxpayers' pockets, the relatively modest number of "truly needy" people expanded to tens of millions of individuals and companies, all pleading "poverty."

The result? Once the first exception to the moral premise was made, it became remarkably easy to keep right on making exceptions. Before long the exceptions became the rule—subsidies to farmers, loans to college students, bailouts for big corporations—and soon the original purported objective was all but forgotten. This tendency to expand on a negative or immoral act can be seen in many other areas of life. Doesn't the drug addict often begin with an innocent puff or two of marijuana? Doesn't the unfaithful spouse start by cheating on his or her mate only reluctantly and sparingly at first? Doesn't the bank robber start out by shoplifting when he's young?

In each example, the early actions of the individuals are somewhat innocent, reluctant, and/or inconsequential, but, almost without exception, they mushroom. So it is with the little white lie. Morality is the concept of right and wrong. You either believe that lying, stealing, cheating, and deceiving are right, or you believe they are wrong. If they are wrong, then they are *never* morally justified.

A good rule I have established for keeping myself from getting lulled into the little-white-lie trap is contained in the *Fishbowl Theory,* which states: Your chances of going to Heaven are directly proportionate to the degree to which you live every moment as though the whole world were watching.

The Rationalization Lie

About ten years ago, as my first book, *Winning Through Intimidation*, was rising to prominence, I was contacted by the publisher of Fawcett Books regarding the licensing of paperback rights. After several days of negotiations, I tentatively agreed to a nice six-figure advance for the sale of these rights. (I say "tentatively," because many of the terms of the licensing arrangement had yet to be discussed.) To lend the proper perspective to this story, I should point out that, at that particular time in my life, the Fawcett offer represented money that I desperately needed. Even though it would not by a long shot solve all of my financial problems, it certainly held the promise of putting out a lot of fires.

As fate would have it, the day after I had verbally accepted the six-figure offer from Fawcett, another paperback publisher called me and offered—Would you believe?—twice as much! I was stunned. In my precarious financial state, it would have been dangerous to tempt me with an offer of just $25,000 more than Fawcett's, let alone an offer that was double theirs. If the first offer would solve a lot of problems, you can imagine what a 100% increase might accomplish.

I found myself trying to rationalize why it would be morally justifiable for me to accept the second publisher's offer. After all, I reasoned, Fawcett and I had not yet agreed on any of the other terms of the deal. And, besides, everyone in the business world knows that a deal isn't a deal until it's in writing, right?

Feeling unsettled by the fact that my mind seemed to be spinning a web of rationalizations that would sanction my accepting the larger offer, I sought the counsel of my friend, Pistol

Pauline, a buyer for a large bookstore chain in New York. Pauline is a savvy publishing executive who possesses an abundance of wisdom, most of it harvested directly from the seeds of experience. Having begun her career the year after Gutenberg invented the printing press, she's been around long enough to have seen it all.

After briefing her on my dilemma, I admitted that I had been toying with some rationalizations for accepting the more lucrative of the two offers. Pistol Pauline was direct: "Kid, publishing is a small industry. Everybody knows everybody else. You're young, and this is only your first book. If you go back on your word to Fawcett, you'll live to regret it. Think long term." I took her advice.

Because of the high stakes involved, this decision constituted a very important turning point for me. It's much easier to do the right thing when there's not much on the line. But this had been a temptation that was almost irresistible. I may not have passed this crucial test with flying colors, but, fortunately for me, I did pass it.

Short term, it hurt a lot. Long term, however, I reaped the rewards. The sums I was able to command on future book deals with Fawcett on the basis of a mere handshake dwarfed the advances that had been discussed in the *Winning Through Intimidation* negotiations. And, instead of giving myself a black eye with the people at Fawcett, which undoubtedly would have become rapidly visible to the rest of the publishing industry, I ended up making a lot of good friends at that company and enjoyed many years of harmonious dealings with them.

The Exaggeration Lie

Exaggeration is really just another form of lying, and I learned the hard way, during my early years in business, that the price of exaggeration is loss of credibility. Nothing makes me lose confidence in a person more quickly than to discover that he's inflated his facts or feats.

I rarely find a tendency toward exaggeration among successful people, which is probably one of the many reasons that they are successful in the first place. I was reminded of this during a recent audience with Black Bart. In a previous discussion, Bart had mentioned to me that he had experienced considerable success drilling for gas in Louisiana—to the tune of proven reserves in the area of $700 million. During the course of a subsequent conversation with him, I happened to allude a couple of times to his "$700-million gas deal."

With a disturbed look on his face, Black Bart interrupted, "You know, I'm a little concerned about the fact that you keep referring to that Louisiana situation as a $700-million deal. I wouldn't want to mislead you. It's true that the proven reserves are $700 million, but that's not *my* share of the profits."

He then went on to explain that the discounted value of the reserves (if he were to sell them today for cash) was about $350 million (he pointed out that it would take about seven years of drilling to get all of the gas out of the ground). Just like that, the $700-million gas deal was cut in half. He then pointed out that the drilling expenses would amount to about $175 million, which left only a paltry $175 million of operating income.

But he still wasn't through. He further explained that the tax bite would be about $75 million, leaving a $100 million profit—of which *his 25% interest* would be worth about $25 million. In other words, the real value of this "$700-million gas deal," from the standpoint of Black Bart's pocketbook, was only $25 million.

Now, we all agree that $25 million is nothing to sneeze at, even if you're Black Bart. But that's not the point. The crucial lesson here is that he did not want me overstating his case by 2700%. I can't say whether this was a morally or pragmatically motivated action on Black Bart's part (or both), but I do know that it was an intelligent action. He did not get where he is by accumulating a closetful of exaggeration skeletons along the way.

Unfortunately, most people are *not* like Black Bart. The average person is not capable of comprehending that exaggeration and lying are synonymous. I always keep this in mind when people start throwing large numbers at me. Here's an example of how you might apply the Black Bart lesson:

Say that a real estate salesman tells you that he makes "about $100,000 a year." "About" probably means that last year he made $88,248.80—and that was in gross commissions! Since most sales commissions are split with another broker, $44,124.40 was probably paid out in co-brokerage fees. The broker who employs the salesman then took half of the net commissions as his cut, which would have left $22,062.20. Figuring in his gas, wear and tear on his car, and other incidental expenses, Mr. About-$100,000-A-Year actually ended up with a grand total of $13,822.53—and that was *last year.* This year, of course, things aren't going nearly as well! While he may drive a gas-guzzling Cadillac and wear shiny tassled loafers, just follow him home some evening and watch him cry as he and his wife pore over the bills piled high on the kitchen table.

Be on the alert for exaggeration lies, at least until a person has proven that he is worthy of your trust. A good rule of thumb to use to reduce an overblown claim down to its bare bones is spelled out in the *Shrink-It-Down-To-Size Theory:* When a person tries to impress you with a boxcar-size income figure, a safe formula to apply is to divide the figure by two; then multiply by one, divide by three, and circle the subtotal in red; wrinkle the paper up in a ball, throw it against the wall, jump up and down on it four times, then straighten it out and put it back on the table; continue—add three, subtract eight, multiply by two, and, finally, divide by five; then, as a measure of insurance, subtract another seven. As simple as that, you've got the guy's *real* income.

The Kindness Lie

A friend of mine, Bobby Beaver, recently made some interesting comments during a philosophical discussion we were having about honesty. He said that he didn't believe in honesty or dishonesty, but, rather, he believed in kindness. He went on to explain,

"But I tell you, Claudine, I made about $100,000 last year.
It's just that my net was only thirteen grand."

"I know how to tell the truth, and I know how not to hurt people, but I don't know how to do both at the same time." He felt there are times when dishonesty can be positive and honesty can be cruel or embarrassing, and his position was that he would rather be kind than honest in certain situations.

If this statement had come from just anyone, I might have dismissed it without a second thought. But Bobby Beaver has built an irreproachable reputation as one of the giants in this country in the field of public relations. From personal experience, I know him to be a basically honest man, so I gave his statements considerable thought.

My conclusion was that the policy of lying out of kindness was unjustified. In almost every case I have found that, by taking the trouble to think the matter through carefully, I can avoid both lying *and* hurting someone's feelings. For example, when I'm too busy to talk to certain people (the reality is that you are sometimes too busy to talk to some people, but not to others), I prefer that my secretary tell them that I'm "tied up right now" (which is *always* true) and will call them back later, rather than lie by saying that I'm not in. Unless that person is neurotic (in which case I *definitely* don't want to speak with him), this shouldn't hurt his feelings—and I've avoided opening the door to a potentially bad habit.

Also, there's the question of whether or not shielding someone from the truth is really a kindness. Since there are an infinite number of situations in which this dilemma could arise, it's impossible to state flatly that it would *never* be in a person's best interest to be lied to. However, it is important not to let an exception spread into moral decay.

I believe that Bobby Beaver is one of those rare souls who *can* make an occasional exception, based on good intentions, without falling victim to the exception trap. Being inherently kind *and* honest, he is, when necessary, able to make a value judgment without compromising his basic belief in honesty. But it's a risky business. The temptation to allow the exception to become the rule is simply too great for most people.

The Omission Lie

Omitting relevant information is one of the most frequently used forms of lying, and one of the most difficult to reconcile philosophically. The guideline I use in trying to determine whether or not something should be "omitted" (i.e., whether or not I should refrain from volunteering certain information) is to ask myself, "Will the other party draw wrong conclusions, and therefore make decisions injurious to himself, because of information that I have not divulged?"

Admittedly, this is a rather general guideline, which is precisely why "lying by omission" is such a difficult subject to deal with. If there is such a thing as "borderline lying," lying by omission is it. On one side of the line, you are leaning in the moral direction of honesty; on the other side, you are leaning toward dishonesty. And, unfortunately, the side of the line on which a person is standing at any given moment is in the eye of the beholder.

If you sell someone a piece of real estate, knowing that the city has plans to condemn it (which you project will bring less than the price you're willing to sell it for), is it your moral obligation to tell the buyer about the possible condemnation before completing the sale? If you want someone to keep you company round trip from Houston to New York, is it your obligation to tell him that you plan to stop off in Chicago on the way back? If you commit to performing a service for someone by a certain date, should you tell him that it may not be your best work because of several other commitments you've already made?

I realize that if you carry this principle to its ultimate extreme, you can go insane. When you sit down to play poker with strangers at a resort, should you tell them that you're an expert player? Before you kiss your date, should you tell her that you have a cold? When a child asks if he can go to the refrigerator to get a soft drink, should he tell his parents that it's the last bottle? Obviously, there's no end to it. It's the one area where you have no choice but to draw lines.

The best guide, as I said, is to ask yourself whether or not the omitted information will cause the other party to make decisions that will be harmful to himself. Beyond that, an even more important rule is: When in doubt, *don't* leave it out.

If all else fails, try the pragmatism of the *Haunted World Theory:* Assume that everyone with whom you have dealings, no matter how casual or trivial those dealings may be, will come back to haunt you at some future date. The cliché that warns us that "it's a small world" is not without basis in my own experience. Every time I unthinkingly slight a person, it seems as if he ends up being the brother-in-law of someone whose blessing I need in a deal I'm working on. You may successfully rationalize an omission to yourself, but always be prepared to face its ghost down the road.

Pragmatically speaking, dishonesty leads to unhappiness and financial failure. Based on the empirical evidence, I sincerely believe that honesty pays, and for good reason: remember, actions have consequences. A dishonest act may occasionally get you out of a short-term jam, but long term it will be costly. The accelerating collapse of Western Civilization is an ominous reminder of how true this is. At first, all of the government's lying, stealing, cheating, and deception seemed to provide a bonanza of false prosperity. But, in time, the natural consequences of all this dishonesty began to surface.

Once I catch a person in a lie, be it a little white lie, an omission, an exaggeration, or any other kind of lie, I am, at the very least, on the alert when dealing with him in the future. How can I be sure at what point he draws his lines? I have often avoided dealing with just such a person, particularly when I have noted little white lies on more than just one occasion. If a man will lie about an unimportant matter, why wouldn't he lie about something that is significant to his well-being? Perhaps he wouldn't, but it would be foolhardy of me to make that assumption.

Think long term! Don't engage in a "convenience" lie just to get out of an uncomfortable situation. The practical problem with the convenience lie is that you won't always be able to remember what you've said. This is the liar's dilemma—trying to remember what he's said and to whom he's said it. It's why the actions of a compulsive liar can sometimes border on slapstick comedy.

The compulsive liar is caught on a pathological merry-go-round. He has told so many lies that he feels compelled to keep telling more and more in an attempt to keep the "whole cloth" from unraveling; but the more he lies, the harder it is to remember everything he has said. As a result, he just keeps digging a deeper hole.

This is the reason that the collapse of Western Civilization is an accelerating phenomenon. Instead of admitting their transgressions, elected officials have trapped themselves in the criminal's Catch-22 box: to cover up their crimes, they must commit *more* crimes. Watergate is a glaring example of this kind of convoluted thinking.

Because actions have consequences, there is only one thing more important than to be perceived as an honest person, and that is to *be* an honest person. Remember, one of the by-products of the moral revolution is the faulty perception of a majority of people. It stands to reason that if a person views a liberal "humanitarian" as honest and honorable, his upside-down view of the world would likely cause him to view a truly honest man as dishonest. If a person views income taxes as a moral necessity, his theft-is-honest moral premise would virtually force him to conclude that corresponding acts of self-defense (such as "tax evasion") are *dishonest*. (Obviously, an act of true self-defense can *never* be dishonest.) By the same token, such a person could not comprehend that every individual who receives a government check—be it in the form of unemployment compensation, Social Security, or a government grant—is committing a crime. The individual who cashes a government check is stealing, *regardless* of whether or not he chooses to acknowledge it as such.

If you've ever been wrongly accused by someone who has his

morals hanging out to dry, you know how frustrating it can be. That's when your *firsthand knowledge* of your own honesty can become a very comforting companion. Honesty does not always make a man popular, but it does make him *free.* Viktor Frankl is right: To choose one's own way is the last of the human freedoms. It makes you feel absolutely clean and free inside to know that you have chosen a strict policy of honesty when it would have been so easy to go along with today's perverse moral standards. Regardless of how others view your actions, you must have faith that, in the long run, truth will triumph. In this vein, the Red Baron handed down the following piece of wisdom to me a couple of years ago, which it is now my pleasure to pass on to you: *If your hands are clean and your cause is just and your requests are reasonable, you have nothing to worry about.*

THE BIG LIARS

Normally, it takes some contact with a person to discern his true moral makeup. You do not, however, have to wait until someone proves himself to be dishonest to be wary of him. There are broad criteria you can use as parameters. For example, there are whole groups of people who can safely be categorized under one heading: Big Liars.

While it's true that any individual in a group may be an exception, you can't afford to give every person you meet an honesty test. The very nature of the bond that unites people in certain groups seems virtually to invite dishonest actions, if not insist upon them. There are four major Big Liar groups, and each of them is highly visible and influential.

These Big Liars have played a major role in precipitating the moral revolution, and they are actively involved in bringing down the remaining structure of Western Civilization. Obviously, it would be in your best interest to have as little contact as possible with people in these groups. Because of their high visibility, however, that may not be totally practical, so it will be up to you not to be influenced by their unprincipled and tortuous actions.

Here, then, are the most visible Big Liars—groups of people whose motives make it virtually impossible for them to be honest for stretches of more than five to ten minutes at a time—groups you must be especially wary of.

Government

By *government,* I am referring to both politicians and so-called bureaucrats. To question the honesty of either politicians or bureaucrats would by now be passé, to say the least. I assume that anyone sophisticated enough to be reading this book already understands that most politicians and their appointees are compulsively dishonest, so it would serve no useful purpose to belabor the point here. Let it just suffice to say that you should not only ignore everything that anyone connected with government says, but, in most instances, and where practical, do the exact *opposite* of what is suggested or demanded.

This is graduate-school stuff we're discussing here, so if you still feel the need to be convinced that these public parasites are larcenous, you're reading the wrong book; I suggest instead that you start from the beginning by reading *Restoring the American Dream.* If that's not to your liking, then you might consider picking up a copy of *Aesop's Fables* and curling up by the fire with a pacifier in your mouth.

Liberals

Just what is a "liberal," anyway? You may have noticed that I've used quotation marks around the word *liberal,* and with good reason. For, you see, a "liberal" does not really exist. He is only a figment of the untested imagination.*

In today's upside-down world, a liberal is variously defined as one who is tolerant, broad-minded, and in favor of reform or

---

* Though quotation marks are appropriate around the word *liberal,* I will, for ease in reading, avoid their use hereafter.

progress. Collectively, these adjectives constitute one of the biggest lies ever told. It's important that you understand the basic lie of so-called liberalism, because a person who can live with this kind of deceit is capable of anything.†

A liberal certainly is neither tolerant of, nor broad-minded about, the beliefs of libertarians, capitalists, or individuals who desire just to "drop out" and be left alone. As to the liberal's idea of reform or progress, it is always *away* from freedom, and certainly away from ownership of what one produces. Instead, his reforms always turn out to favor mob rule, i.e., rule through government intervention, which is usually brought about through the ballot box when a majority states its desire to violate the rights of a minority. Above all, a liberal's idea of progress *always* calls for taking (by force, if necessary) from those *he* deems to be "rich" and passing the booty along to those *he* deems to be "poor."

And who, exactly, are "the poor"? Like liberals, "the poor" do not really exist; they are a figment of the *liberal's* imagination! They are a hallucination that liberals also sometimes refer to as "the underprivileged" or "the truly needy."

"Poor" is not an absolute term. No one can be classified as being either rich or poor. Every person in the world is poorer than some people and richer than others. The question, as Ayn Rand pointed out many years ago, is still the same: Who shall decide? Who shall decide who is poor? Who shall decide how much should be given to them? Who shall decide from whom the loot will be extorted?

The answer today, of course, is that *everyone* decides! Just about everyone now claims to be "poor." It's a stampede! Every

---

†Throughout this book, whenever the term *liberal* is used, I am referring to those who today *claim* to be liberals. Likewise, when referring to *liberalism,* I mean the ideology of today's self-proclaimed liberals. It should, however, be noted that today's liberals bear no ideological or philosophical relationship whatsoever to the original American colonial liberals, who would now be more appropriately described as "libertarians."

man for himself! Anything goes! From Chrysler Corporation to food-stamp recipients, from rent-control beneficiaries to the National Savings and Loan League, everyone is frantically filling out the forms to qualify as "truly needy." And why not—they've found that it works! In fact, as it turns out, "the poor" ends up being everyone but *you*.

This, of course, is not to say that there are not many people in Western countries who are far worse off than others. That's what life has always been about; that's what life will always be about. There must always be a bottom third in any free (or semi-free) society. Poverty is a natural consequence of ignorance, incompetence, and/or laziness. And well it should be. The threat of negative consequences is what keeps people striving to learn more, to improve their skills, and to work harder. And that makes for a healthy society.

Speaking of the liberal's creation of "the poor," this is a good place to unmask a very important misconception—the generally accepted notion that a liberal is altruistic. The problem with that proposition is that—here we go again—altruism does not really exist. When a person claims to be sacrificing for someone, the fact is that he is making a free choice. No matter how he protests to the contrary, he is choosing to do the thing that *he* wants to do. While it may be an unpleasant choice, the fact remains that it is *his* choice.

Once and for all: A liberal is *not* altruistic; he is *not* tolerant; he is *not* broad-minded; he is *not* in favor of true reform or progress (i.e., reform or progress *toward* freedom). Therefore, liberalism is, in every respect, a lie. That is why you will never hear a liberal argument based on fact or logic.

So who are all these people who willingly saddle themselves with this tag? I have wrestled with this fascinating question over a long period of time. It is truly baffling on its surface, because, having seen liberals in action and knowing what they stand for, the question is, why would anyone *want* to be known as a liberal?

To understand the workings of this group, one must break it down into its component parts, for there is not just one kind of liberal, but five. They include:

1. *Uninformed liberals* (hereinafter referred to as "blank-libs").
2. *Ignorant liberals* (hereinafter referred to as "dumblibs").
3. *Confused liberals* (hereinafter referred to as "fluster-libs").
4. *Phony liberals* (hereinafter referred to as "fakelibs").
5. *Malevolent liberals* (hereinafter referred to as "true-libs").

I remind you again that *none* of these liberals is altruistic. Each acts in what he believes to be his own best interests at all times. Beyond that, however, there are major differences among them. Let's examine them individually and see what they are.

Blanklibs. Most liberals are simply uninformed. One of the clear signs of the disintegration of the Western world is that few people bother to read, and, of those who do, most read only publications that actually print *dis*information. Everyone, of course, watches television, whose disinformation is even worse than that of the print media. If the extent of one's knowledge comes from what he sees and hears on television and reads in local newspapers and major magazines, the unfortunate fact is that he cannot help but to be uninformed—with a liberal tilt. The reality is that few people have even heard of the great economic and philosophy books of our time, let alone read them, and only a brave little army of rational thinkers takes the trouble to read alternative publications such as hard-money newsletters.

I would not want you to infer, however, that it's just the lower and middle classes who produce this gargantuan army of blanklibs. Some of the most information-starved liberals I've met have come from the highest income brackets. The entertainment industry, for example, is infested with blanklibs. Anyone who has watched an Ed Asner stumble incoherently through some liberal exhortation on television certainly knows what I mean. While ramblings of this kind often bring hostile charges from freedom advocates, I believe that in most cases such charges are misplaced. If you listen closely to the erratic, inconsistent, and/or irrational statements of entertainment-industry types such as this, it becomes obvious that they are simply uninformed.

Experience has taught me that it is futile to try to convert blanklibs to a life of reason. The chances of getting such people to read and think are extremely slim. It happens occasionally, but I would not want to have my life or assets depend on it.

Dumblibs. Ignorant liberals are just that—ignorant. They are the millions of people who simply are not intelligent enough to understand the facts even when exposed to them. They do not have the mental capacity to see that liberalism is immoral and contradictory. As with uninformed liberals, it is unlikely that any amount of effort on your part will save them.

From what I have observed, combined with what I've heard from others who are in a better position to judge, Ted Kennedy would probably qualify as the archetypical ignorant liberal. While I'm not trying to underplay his obvious rich-kid's guilt complex, I believe that his utter inability to absorb information or to grasp the facts overrides any curable, psychological problem. Kennedy, after all, was the first presidential candidate in history who, when asked on national television why he wanted to be president, could not think of an answer! Now that's what you call hard-core dumb.

In fact, it was Ted Kennedy who first inspired the question in my mind, Why do we have only a Hall of Fame? Where is it written that we should not have a Hall of Dumb? Or a Hall of Mean? Or a Hall of Blah? I would like to go on record, here and now, as nominating Ted Kennedy as the initial inductee into the Hall of Dumb.

Flusterlibs. By a *confused liberal,* I am referring to someone who is informed (which usually means he is not ignorant), yet still persists in believing the liberal myths. By *liberal myths,* I mean such confused thinking as: poverty can be erased simply by stealing from producers and giving the heist to nonproducers; if a select group of men (politicians) is given the power to make moral choices for others, it will do so without abusing that power; equality is not only possible, but desirable; and on and on and on ad nauseum. Giving him the posthumous benefit of the doubt, I might be inclined to dub Hubert Humphrey as a good example of a flusterlib.

The flusterlib seems never to take note of reality. He totally disregards history, which clearly tells him that so-called liberalism inevitably results in making "the poor" poorer. He does not even attempt to test his premises on a moral basis, because that leads only to contradiction, which in turn leads to still more confusion.

It is interesting to note that the largest group of libertarian converts comes from intelligent, informed flusterlibs. The prime age range is 25 to 35. Reading the right books, talking to rational people, and, most important, observing the realities of the world in which we live, is what ends up doing it for them. Before the age of twenty-five, they haven't had enough time for the untried rhetoric of their college professors to have worn off, and after thirty-five stubbornness and fatigue tend to set in.

Fakelibs.   Whereas I can sympathize with someone who is uninformed, ignorant, or confused, I find phony liberals to be reprehensible. If they would just come right out and admit that they don't give a hoot about "the poor," you might be able to conjure up a little respect for them. However, you can be sure that they will never make such an admission, because their long suit is pragmatism. They are masters at understanding that success or failure, especially in politics, can very much depend upon one's ability to avoid mixing his personal beliefs with what he says in public.

Franklin D. Roosevelt was perhaps in a class by himself among phony liberals. Historians have by now so successfully unmasked his uncanny ability to do and say whatever was politically popular at the moment that even the most die-hard New Dealers

"A genuine super-dummy. Golly, he's awesome."

admit that FDR was not averse to engaging in a little shading of the truth now and then.

For example, when an anti-lynching bill was introduced into Congress, FDR made a momentous political decision not to support it. In 1958, his wife, Eleanor, explained the matter, saying that FDR had decided not to vote for the anti-lynching bill because he needed the southern votes to back him in the war effort, and he was afraid that he wouldn't get them if he supported such a bill.

Another example of the true Roosevelt was his refusal to override the immigration quotas when shiploads of German Jews arrived on the shores of the United States in the late 1930's, even though he was well aware of Hitler's persecution practices. It has been estimated that, as a result of FDR's lack of compassion in this matter, the majority of those Jews ended up dying in Nazi gas chambers.

Of course, it would be naive to believe that the actions of fakelibs are motivated only by pragmatism. A fakelib also usually suffers from delusions of benevolence, righteousness, and magnanimity. He longs to be loved. Unfortunately, however, his phony humanitarian objectives prove disastrous to the lowest income earners, because his chief source of ego gratification is the person who needs his help. That's what motivates him to perpetuate the greatest of all deceits. He does not want those at the bottom level of society to be too well off, for where would he be without them? If their lot were to improve, they would no longer need his help!

Truelibs.   Finally, we come to the malevolent liberal—the only person who can rightfully be called a *true* liberal. This is the individual whose intentions are truly evil. More often than not, his actions have their roots in the ugly soil of envy.

Examples of persons who appear to be malevolent liberals would be Ralph Nader and Tom Hayden (the Hall of Mean?). Men like these are not in search of equal well-being for all people. Their objective is equal misery! This kind of sadistic outlook is usually the result of an individual's unhappiness with his own status in life, which tends to carry with it a lack of self-worth and self-esteem.

In reality, the fact that a person may call himself a liberal is irrelevant. He might just as well call himself a "socialist" or "communist," because, in the final analysis, all three of these banners advertise a belief in *compulsory compassion,* which necessitates a belief in the morality of sacrificing the rights of some individuals to the so-called good of others. Liberals accomplish this end through "majority rule," while communists accomplish the same end through "temporary" dictatorships—that always turn out to be permanent. (Socialists apparently are some strange mixture of the two, but no one seems to be quite sure.)

It is therefore important that *you* not be fooled by labels. A more appropriate name to describe all three—liberals, socialists, and communists alike—would be "theftists," because all three share a deep-seated belief in the morality of theft. Underneath all their benevolent propaganda, they tenaciously adhere to the perversity of this position.

On reflection, there probably is one distinction that can be made among a liberal, socialist, and communist. While all three are dishonest, each one presents himself differently to the world. A liberal is nothing more than a closet communist; a socialist is in the process of coming out of the closet; and a communist is already on the outside, *trying to shove you into the closet.*

But the important thing for you to remember is that *all* liberals are dangerous. Dispel the notion that liberals are well-meaning. They are *not* well-meaning. While you may be able to make a good argument that some blanklibs, dumblibs, and flusterlibs have good intentions (by some standards), it is still difficult to see the goodness in using force against people who are not interfering in the lives of others. For that is what really lies at the heart of the liberal's activities—the use of force against those who refuse to go along with his ideas and demands.

The reality is that all liberals are dangerous; they shoot to kill! If you don't believe this, just refuse to obey one of their laws of aggression (i.e., aggression against *you*), then follow through by trying to defend yourself when they attempt to *force* you to obey. You will very quickly find out just how benevolent liberals are.

The Media

The people who own, operate, and work for radio and television stations, newspapers, and magazines are motivated by virtually the same objectives as politicians—they are out to win "votes." If people like what a newscaster has to say, they cast their vote by watching him every evening, which helps to increase his network's profits. On the other hand, if too many people do not like a newscaster, they, in effect, vote him out of a job by merely switching channels.

Obviously, then, it pays media people to say things that are popular. And what has been most popular throughout every age and throughout every area of the world is to tell people that they *deserve* more of everything; that they have a *right* to more of everything; that it is the government's duty to see to it that they *receive* more of everything.

Say what sells! Anything that will keep the minds of the masses occupied—and away from any kind of serious thinking— is useful. As in *Brave New World*, give the people their somas. Keep them laughing, crying, excited, hating the enemy—anything—just keep them occupied, and in line, at all costs. This means not only guilt- and envy-oriented news stories, but also Monday Night Football, sitcoms geared toward a third-grade intellectual level, trumped-up crises, and sensationalism. This is the stuff that works!

What *doesn't* work for the media is to call upon the many rational, intelligent, economic experts in this country who have a clear understanding of the fiscal realities that are bankrupting the Western world. True prophets have never been too popular, mainly because people do not take kindly to predictions that they are about to be punished for their larcenous ways. This makes it rather easy for the government and its media pawns. In fact, in

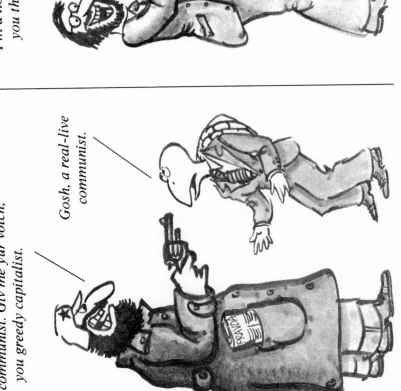

addition to the regular media "experts," Washington maintains a sort of standing army, on call at all times, to fight these blasphemous prophets. I affectionately refer to this powerful, ignorant, and morally corrupt army of economic puppets as "Galbraithians."

Whenever any of the great economic minds of our time—men like Douglas Casey, Friedrich A. Hayek, and Murray Rothbard—begins to make the slightest inroad into the minds of average citizens, the liberalist media simply open their magazines, newspapers, television networks, and radio stations to the Galbraithians, who are thus given free access into American homes. They quickly assure the public that the forecasts of these "alarmists" are nonsense. Such assurances are quite effective, thank you, since the true economic prophets *have no corresponding means of responding on a mass basis.*

Throughout history, the following sequence of events has repeated itself over and over again, yet the majority of people seem oblivious to it: First, men of wisdom warn of a coming cataclysm, and, in response, Galbraithians assure the public that "it could never happen here" or "it could never happen today." Second, the masses begin to regurgitate these assurances to one another until the phenomenon feeds on itself. Anyone who then calls attention to the obvious realities is labeled a "doomsayer" and ignored. Third, the cataclysmic event comes to pass!

This three-step cycle has been observed in nation after nation with monotonous repetition. All three steps were clearly followed in ancient Rome, in pre-Napoleonic France of the 1790's, in Russia prior to the Bolshevik Revolution in 1917, and in Germany under Hitler's early rule. Notwithstanding the lessons of history, men and women prefer to cling to folly and accept the assurances of the Galbraithians rather than face up to the forces that are destroying their lives.

That is why you can expect the Galbraithian chorus of assurances to continue, even in the face of obvious disaster. Remember this time-tested reality: *People do not want to hear the truth.* They have become too accustomed to their false prosperity. They desperately need someone to tell them that all is well, and, such being the case, the Galbraithians do fill a rather important need.

Unfortunately for all of us, however, you cannot change reality simply by ignoring it; you cannot make it go away with the ploy of a casual dismissal; you cannot defuse it just by making fun of those who call the public's attention to it.

The media have still other ways of winning popularity contests. When they aren't reporting on some natural disaster like an earthquake, flood, hurricane, or Jane Fonda, one of their favorite lies is the made-to-order "crisis." And, like the government, they think nothing of spending tens of millions of dollars to manufacture a single event.

One such event was the recent "Falklands crisis," which Argentine author Jorge Luis Borges characterized as "a fight between two bald men over a comb." Since I have great respect for the media's ability to agitate viewers' nervous systems on cue, I must conclude that they were particularly desperate for news during this Laurel and Hardy event.

The part I loved best was at the outset, when it was announced that the British militia had been dispatched to the Falklands and would arrive in *two to three weeks.* I mean, it was Hanna-Barbera stuff. The British, having long since been relegated to the status of a second-rate power, reacted like an overjoyed bully who had just bumped into a 99-pound weakling.

Judging from the number of troops and equipment England sent to the Falklands, you would have thought they were preparing to take Iwo Jima. To this day, it's not clear in my mind whether or not Argentina even has an army or navy. While the Western world's media darlings were saturating citizens with information about the "Falklands crisis," one seriously wondered whether the handful of sheepherders on those tiny, heretofore unheard-of islands even knew that anything unusual was going on.

Crises, though, are extraordinary events. It's the everyday stream of lies and deception that the media generates that continually warps the minds of Mr. and Mrs. America. Their explanations of inflation are false; their unemployment figures are false (for starters, they don't include government employees, who are, in effect, unemployed); their stories about the suffering of "the poor and needy" are false; their past insistences that everything was fine with Social Security, savings and loans, and the housing industry were false (this is put in the past tense, because the cold facts have virtually forced them to admit that there may, in fact, be "a few problems" in these areas); their presentations of virtually all major issues—especially economic issues—are false.

And don't forget an important adjunct to the media—advertising. Remember, advertisers are out to win votes for the exact same reasons as the media.

The biggest brainwashers are Merrill Lynch's "bullish on America" ads. Forget record interest rates. Forget sky-high unemployment. Forget widespread bankruptcies of major corporations. I tell you, Merrill Lynch is bullish on America! The facts don't matter, folks; everything is going to be fine, because Merrill Lynch says so. Just contact your nearest Merrill Lynch Equity Management office to see if you can qualify for a second or third mortgage on your already overvalued home.

This is a prime example of how listening to Big Liars can get you into trouble. Whenever I see the likes of a Merrill Lynch, Visa, or American Express tempting people to get further into debt, I feel as though we're living in one big garden of Eden—and I don't think I need to suggest who the serpent is.

Perhaps in a class by themselves, though, when it comes to false representations, are the ads soliciting recruits for the army and navy. Uncle Sam has gone Madison Avenue; his ads are now slick. To watch them on television, you'd think that the only guys who qualify for the military are preppies from Harvard and Yale. Apart from their questionable clean-cut images, the youngsters in the ads look like they're having a ball, which makes for light comedy for anyone who has actually been there.

Finally, the media dispense some of their biggest lies in the form of sensationalism. Whether presenting patently false information or just distorting the facts, the objective is to hook the public into thinking that a story is "juicy." Unfortunately, I can speak firsthand about the effectiveness of sensationalism, because

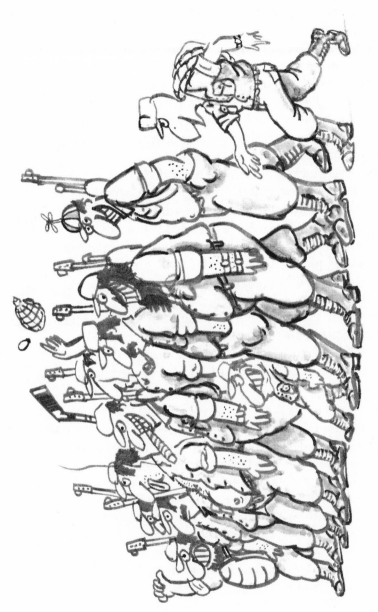

"All right, you guys, look sharp—we're on television."
♪♪ *Be—all that you can be—in the ar-r-r-my.* ♪♪♪

I've been the target of such distortions more often than I care to remember.

You may have seen the results of one incident several years ago. *Time* magazine wanted to do a feature article about me and said they needed a good picture to go with the article. They proceeded to send a photographer to my office, who ended up taking a couple of hundred pictures. With that many shots from which to select, I fully expected them to choose the one that came closest to making me look like Errol Flynn.

No such luck. The dice were loaded from the start. When the shooting session began, the photographer had said to me, "Why don't we just try to loosen you up a bit? Just fool around; make some funny faces. Here, let's see you make a fist—like this (he demonstrated what he had in mind). Yeah, that's right—a fist. Good. How about a few facial contortions (he again demonstrated). I've found that this type of thing helps to loosen up my subjects."

Without giving it much thought, I tried to relax and go along with the "loosening up" part of the picture-taking session. I joked around with the photographer and made a few fists and funny faces for him. Little did I know that the rest of the session was purely cosmetic; he had already gotten the pictures he wanted!

Within a couple of weeks, there I was in *Time*, sporting a gruff sneer and clenching my fist. I just happened to be looking to my left in the center of a two-page spread. Juxtaposed was a picture of Michael Korda, the author of *Power!*, looking to his right. Needless to say, he was also clenching a fist and staring ominously at me. A nice piece of photo editing, to say the least. Dishonest, but clever. I'm sure there wasn't a *Time* reader in the country who didn't think that Korda's and my pictures were taken in concert, and that we willingly—even eagerly—posed that way for the article. Alas, the truth is that Korda and I had never met. But the idea was "sensational"—two obvious "bad guys" making fists at one another. The content of the story, need I point out, was even more misleading.

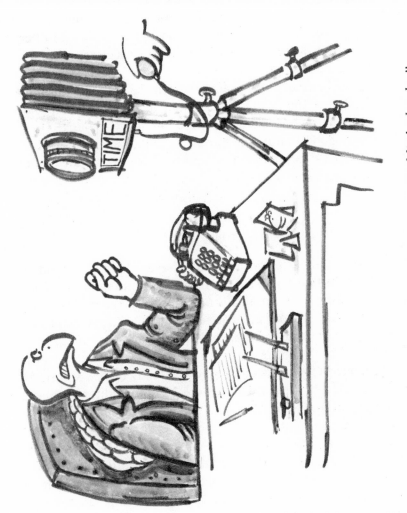

"That's right—just make a fist. That's a good little dumbo."

Early hoaxes like this helped to firmly implant in the public's mind the ruse of "Ringer the Intimidator." It's not something you cherish, but ultimately you learn to live with it. Your mother, your friends, your business associates, and your readers know better, which is a consolation you learn to be thankful for. It's an interesting irony that the media themselves find it necessary to be dishonest in order to create "bad guys."

As the effects of the collapse worsen, be wary of the most visible Big Liar—the media. They're out to win votes, and to do so they will continue to hand out more and more somas to try to make us feel good—situation comedies, sensationalism, misleading advertising, deceptive and outrightly false news. They know the formula works, so why change?

Attorneys

What can I say about Legalman that I haven't said before? As it is, he complains that I've been too harsh with him in my writings, and perhaps he's right. In all fairness, it's only about 97% of attorneys who are dishonest, negligent, and/or incompetent, yet they make a bad name for the whole profession.

And the profession is growing at an awesome rate. In the United States, Legalman's numbers are already up to a whopping 617,000, compared with Japan's mere 12,000. California alone, that premier example of a modern socialist state, has 79,000 of the nasty little varmints. That's one for every 310 people, compared to Japan's ratio of one to every 9,800. Not to worry, though. If Japan continues its rapid march toward "Westernization," it will eventually catch up, because today's Western society boasts massive webs of laws and regulations imposed on individuals and corporations. And the more massive they get in Japan, the more demand there will be for Legalman's services.

This whole process is quite understandable, once you analyze Legalman's cozy setup. He not only argues the law in court, he also *makes* the law and decides where and how it should be applied. Lawyers are lawyers; judges are lawyers; and well over half of all U.S. Congressmen are lawyers. If ever there was a fix, this is it.

Bolstered by the incestuous partnership between government and the legal profession, Legalman is vested with a unique right—the right to do as he pleases to regular citizens (i.e., those not connected with government or the legal profession). Only a small percentage of today's mesmerized populace is aware of the fact that Legalman, in the course of his work, can say virtually anything he pleases, both in legal briefs and in the courtroom. He can make wild accusations and dispense totally false information, without fear of fine or punishment. Further, he can inundate judges and juries with irrelevancies, hearsay, and other "inadmissible" chatter, knowing full well that his remarks will be absorbed *even if they are declared inadmissible.*

In the past ten years, I have had the misfortune of being involved in court litigation on two occasions. In each instance the presiding judge, while seemingly intelligent and objective concerning all other matters, allowed Legalpunk (a transitory stage between the ranks of Legalboy and Legalman, as explained later in this chapter) to prattle on endlessly about the fact that I had written a book called *Winning Through Intimidation*—even though that had nothing whatsoever to do with the matter being tried!

In the first case, Legalpunk marched around the courtroom, waving a copy of the book in the air, and rambled on about how "it would be a travesty if this man were allowed to use the methods set forth in this book in a court of law." The judge, obviously never having read the book, had little way of knowing that its very theme was to explain to the reader how to defend himself against the exact kind of intimidation that Legalpunk was at that moment practicing! After ruling against me, he later told my attorney (in private, of course) that even though he had realized there was no concrete evidence to support the other side's case, he had decided to give them "the benefit of the doubt."

In the second case, Legalpunk stood at a podium and read

aloud to the courtroom selected excerpts from my book—*out of context*. At no time did the judge make any attempt to put a halt to this circus stunt, let alone rule it inadmissible. This being my second experience of this kind, I became convinced that the only way I could ever hope to receive a fair trial in the future was to find a way to have the *entire* text of *Winning Through Intimidation* read into the court record. If that were accomplished, I would be happy to rest my case. My first choice, however, is to stay out of courtrooms.

If a civilian witness were to say some of the things I've heard come out of Legalman's mouth in court, you can be sure that he would promptly find himself indicted for perjury. But the worst Legalman can expect for repeatedly pelting the courtroom with outrageous remarks is a patronizing chuckle from his fellow attorney, the judge. Bertrand Russell described this shameless situation quite accurately, and poetically, this way:

> Whoever invented the phrase "the naked truth" had perceived an important connection. Nakedness is shocking to all right-minded people, and so is truth. . . . Whenever it has been my ill fortune to be present in court during the hearing of a case about which I had some first-hand knowledge, I have been struck by the fact that no crude truth is allowed to penetrate within those august portals. The truth that gets into a law court is not the naked truth but the truth in court dress, with all its less decent portions concealed. . . . If you wish to mention in a law court any unassimilable fact, you will find that it is contrary to the laws of evidence to do so, and that not only the judge and the opposing counsel but also counsel on your own side will prevent the said fact from coming out.

If you're holding out hope that the situation is going to improve, forget it. It's getting worse every year. These cockroaches in three-piece suits breed rapidly, and they are now immune to all known insecticides. At the rate that Legalboy—the cub attorney—is being turned out (over 5,000 a year in California alone), one can envision the day when there will be more lawyers than clients.

"Your honor, I'd bet my lollipop that this tortoise is trying to use his intimidation methods on this court."

There now seem to be law schools on every street corner. Not the quaint old ivy-covered buildings you pictured as a kid, but tacky-looking structures that appear to be converted army-navy surplus stores or supermarkets. If you can scrape together enough money to buy the minimum required equipment—an $89.95 three-piece polyester suit and a cheap vinyl briefcase—you can qualify. Of course, it also helps to sport an outrageous moustache or beard.

After this silly-looking organism obtains his Legalboy diploma, he is then only a couple of steps from the next plateau. Once he proves that he is incapable of constructing an intelligible, coherent sentence and learns the basic nuances of fee building, he is eligible for graduation to the status of (sound the trumpets): *Legalpunk.*

Legalboy's elevation to the exalted status of Legalpunk (sometimes unofficially referred to as a legal mitzvah) is reminiscent of a bar mitzvah in that he rakes in all the gifts (in the form of fees); unlike a bar mitzvah, however, all the guests (clients) get circumcised! Some day, if all goes well, Legalpunk can trade in his polyester suit for the real thing and earn the ultimate rank of Legalman. But that's easier said than done. To rightfully carry the title, there is much to learn—most of it dishonest.

The most important qualifying skill is legalized extortion. This is accomplished by threatening a company with long, drawn-out litigation. To the degree Legalman has a proven track record (of troublemaking), his threats will be successful. If all goes well, the target of the threats will, in effect, buy off Legalman in order to avoid the time, trouble, aggravation, and expense of a lengthy legal entanglement.

Of course, if the intended victim does not agree to the buyout, Legalman must be prepared to follow through. The objective is then to wear the victim down through delays, harassment, and, hopefully, tying up an important venture. This is accomplished through such fee-building and delay-causing devices as interrogatories, depositions, amended petitions, repetitious requests for irrelevant documents, and other similar gimmicks.

The ultimate is reached when Legalman hooks up with his partner in crime, Uncle Sam, and uses these tactics in a government-brought suit against a major corporation, with a preference toward "antitrust." The frivolous case brought against IBM by the Justice Department is now a classic, a model for all aspiring Legalpunks to study. In that particular case, after thirteen years of preparation and litigation, and the accumulation of *66 million pages* of documents, the Justice Department finally admitted that the suit was "without merit" and dropped it.

Not every attorney, however, manages to work his way up to the big-money cases. Most just settle for perpetrating the normal, day-to-day frauds.* A rather nice market that has opened up for the seedier, small-time counselors is the filing of Social Security disability claims for people. It's getting to be such a lucrative business that there now exists an official organization for these not-above-stooping-to-anything characters. It is straightforwardly called the National Organization of Social Security Claims Representatives, and it has grown from zero to 13,000 attorneys in just two years.

These sleazy humanoids specialize in winning Social Security disability claims for clients, and they usually receive about 25% of the stolen money as their fee. In 1974, the Social Security Administration paid $6 million in attorney fees for 9,000 claimants; in 1981, the figures had zoomed to $65.2 million and 59,000 claimants. *The Wall Street Journal* recently referred to Social Security disability law as a "growth industry." And, in a rare moment of honesty for Legalman, the executive director of this new theft organization admitted, "Obviously it's a lawyers' field day."

Of course, among themselves, attorneys admit that much of

---

*The use of such words as *fraud, stolen money,* and *theft* in the following paragraphs quite obviously is based on my long-standing opinion that the entire Social Security system is an economic fraud, but there is no question that, under current law and current ethical standards of the legal profession, the actions of NOSSCR attorneys are neither illegal nor unethical. Needless to say, however, from a moral standpoint I strongly disagree with both current law in this area and the ethical standards of the legal profession.

the work they do, particularly the frivolous fee-building paper-work, is a farce, but they have no qualms about producing it since "the system" is designed for such nonsense. Every now and then, however, one of their members gets a little frisky and un-thinkingly says something in public that creates embarrassment. Like Melvin Belli's opining that "50% of trial lawyers are incompetent." Or Chief Justice Warren E. Burger's saying that he believes that lawyers generally overcharge their clients, especially for simple transactions, and that law schools and bar associations neglect professional ethics.

For those of us who understand Legalman's neat little setup, it would be a dream come true to see him held civilly and criminally liable for his actions, both in and out of the courtroom. At first, he would be sued and sent to prison at a breakneck pace. Then, as he finally came to accept his fate, Legalman would have no choice but to stop harassing private citizens with meaningless, lie-loaded documents. Further, he would be forced to stop wasting the court's time with fancy legalese and outright perjury.

Can this dream ever become a reality? Only that Big Judge in the Sky can decide. But can we trust Him? What if He wears a three-piece suit and carries a vinyl briefcase?

Politicians and bureaucrats, liberals, media personnel, and attorneys are not the only Big Liars, to be sure, but they are the most visible. And, because they have such easy access to your eyes and ears, you should be extra cautious about overexposure to them. They can irreparably harm you if you allow them to influence your actions. I guess the ultimate destructive force would be a *liberal attorney* who becomes a *politician,* then ends up as a *newscaster* after leaving public office. Even Darth Vader would be no match for such a creature.

But don't allow my flattering treatise on the Big Liars to cause you to ignore the moral condition of the *average person* in today's environment. Unfortunately, he, too, will lie, steal, cheat, and deceive, without ever admitting his actions to himself. On the contrary, because he has grown up during the collapse of Western

Civilization, he is likely to see a dishonest action as *honest*. Remember, he is morally standing on his head, and he has been placed in that position by the planners of the welfare state. It's all right to be sympathetic toward him, on the theory that he knows not what he does, but for goodness' sake stay out of his way!

There is much happiness and success to be found in relationships with other people, but they must be the *right* people. Don't allow the lure of short-term satisfaction (including short-term profits) to tempt you to become involved with those of a different moral persuasion. In the long term, it will bring you nothing but grief.

Most important, keep your *own* house clean, even if it makes you a "square" in today's anything-goes world. Don't be deluded into believing that others are getting ahead of you by being dishonest. Whatever success such people may occasionally experience is usually short term. And even if a dishonest person's success gives the appearance of being long term, it is very likely that he will never achieve *happiness*. In any event, I am still of the opinion that any person who made $1 by being dishonest could have made $2 by being honest.

Constantly monitor your own actions for moral slippage. Test yourself. Submit to relentless self-policing. Refuse to compromise where your honesty is at stake. Always be sure that your hands are clean and your cause is just and your demands are reasonable, and you'll have nothing to worry about. If the Red Baron says it, it must be so.

CHAPTER VI

Eye of the Tiger

Notable for its absence during the ongoing collapse of Western Civilization is the quality of self-discipline. By *self-discipline*, I mean strict adherence to the principle of doing the right thing rather than the instinctive thing. By the *right thing*, I am referring to the action that, at any given time, will bring you the greatest *long-term* success.

The most convincing evidence that the Devil is alive and well on planet Earth is the fact that many of the things we instinctively desire are the very things that are most detrimental to our long-term health, happiness, and success. Therefore, the person who aspires to health, happiness, and success has no choice but to wage a perpetual battle against the temptation to take the easy way out, to grab the immediate benefit, to ignore the potential consequences of his actions. It is a battle that most people today are losing—badly.

It's not surprising that self-discipline is a vanishing trait, for it is in direct conflict with the basic philosophy of an anything-goes society. When you believe you can get anything you want, whenever you want it, where is the need for so painful an art? Self-discipline is old-fashioned. Given that our rulers in Washington are themselves totally lacking in self-discipline, how can it possibly be of any importance? Did not their lack of self-discipline bring us the modern welfare state? Yes, and with it the collapse of Western Civilization!

With that reminder, I repeat: The most certain road to success is to do the *opposite* of that which causes failure. But, as always, most people have instead chosen to *emulate* government, which is just one more reason why they are badly failing. However, very few people are consciously aware that their lack of success is due at least in part to a lack of self-discipline, because it is difficult to analyze the results of the *absence* of a quality. Having grown up in a world where self-discipline is seldom observed, it is a way of life to which few people can relate.

There is nothing quite so pitiful as the individual who lacks control over his own actions. He who bases his life primarily on instinctive actions is, in that respect, on a level with the beasts of the forest. The actions of animals center around expediency; their interests lie in the immediate benefit. How sad that the vast majority of human beings choose to live in a manner that is characteristic of animals.

If you aren't able to control your instinctive actions—if you do not develop a substantial degree of self-discipline—you can fully expect to be swept along by the anything-goes tidal wave that has enveloped our society, and to end up crashing against the rocks of despair along with most of your well-deserving neighbors. If, on the other hand, you become proficient at the art of doing the right thing rather than the instinctive thing, the odds of your achieving your objectives are overwhelmingly on your side. If you sincerely desire to improve your self-discipline, you *can;* it's all in the mind. No special talent is needed; practice is.

To be self-disciplined requires the following: 1) honest evaluation of costs; 2) future-oriented thinking; 3) consistency; and 4) determination.

HONEST EVALUATION OF COSTS

As I pointed out earlier, one of the objectives of this book is to help you to answer three questions, one of which is "What will it (what you want out of life) cost me?" This question does not just apply to one major goal, but to day-to-day desires as well. Anything that is worthwhile in your life—no matter how seemingly insignificant to others—requires an investment of time, energy, pain, and/or sacrifice, the size of the investment being commensurate with the value of the expected benefits. I realize that these are fighting words in today's age of "entitlements," but, alas, they are true. The proof can be seen in the fact that people's "entitlements" (i.e., the goods and services they have been receiving without a corresponding investment of time, energy, pain, and/or sacrifice) are rapidly slipping away from them.

Exercise is a good example of the importance of cost analysis in day-to-day life, because the cost of a serious exercise program is enormous. Jogging is an exercise that most people can relate to, because of its increase in popularity over the past ten years. Anyone who has jogged (I am speaking here of serious jogging, not "social jogging") for a number of years knows that there is no such thing as a "free jog." Every time you leave the house to jog, there's a big, green son-of-a-gun—known to all runners as the Jolly Green Jogger—standing just outside your door, with a changemaker hooked to his belt.

The Jolly Green Jogger is an unmerciful, almost sadistic character, who thinks only in terms of profit and loss. (How appalling!) Before he lets you take even one stride, he demands advance payment—in *four* currencies. He insists that you pay him in time, energy, pain, and sacrifice. There's no negotiating. You pay, or you don't jog.

Supposedly the Jolly Green Jogger was actually jolly at one time, but that predates my own jogging days. Legend has it that, to his dismay, some overly enthusiastic jogger once started the rumor that after you get the hang of jogging, it feels great. As this notion was passed from jogger to jogger, it ultimately evolved into one of the Three Biggest Lies, to wit: "Once you get used to jogging, you experience a relaxed, euphoric, almost trancelike state." Sure you do. About the same euphoric state that you experience when going to the dentist.

The Jolly Green Jogger, somewhat paranoid, takes this lie as a personal affront. He thinks it makes him look soft. And that's why he never lets *anyone* have a free jog. Question: Have you *ever* seen a jogger smiling? A jogger's expressions range from glazed stares, at best, to grimaces of pain. If you intend to become a serious jogger, the Jolly Green Jogger wants you to get it out of your mind that it will eventually feel good. It won't. Some steps hurt *less* than others, but no step feels *good*. There is no joy in jogging! The joy comes after you've finished—*after* you've showered and dressed. That's when you reap the mental and physical benefits you paid for in advance.

Payment in advance is required for anything in life that produces a benefit. Children should be taught this truth at an early age, but few are. If you confront your child about watching television on a school night (which few parents today would dare to do), he will likely plead the old standby line: "I've already done all my homework." The child who says this is not really being truthful, because no child has ever, in the truest sense of the word, done *all* his homework.

An analogy would be my saying that I've done all my work at the office. No one *ever* does "all his work," because there is no limit to how much one can do. The idea that one has done all of one's work, which implies that he has done everything he can possibly do to succeed, is unhealthy. It leads little people (both children and mental dwarfs) to believe that the price of success is considerably less than it really is.

A self-disciplined person understands the reality of the *I've-Done-All-My-Homework Theory:* The only people who have done all their "homework" are dead people. Live people who believe they've done all their homework are individuals who do not have a realistic grasp of what it takes to succeed. Whether it's schoolwork, exercise, or making money, you must pay—*and pay, and pay, and pay*—in terms of time, energy, pain, and/or sacrifice. There is, however, an alternative: failure.

"No, shorty, I don't accept credit cards. What do you think I am, a department store?"

FUTURE-ORIENTED THINKING

As it relates to self-discipline, the future can mean one hour from now; it can mean tomorrow; it can mean next year; or it can mean several years from today. Whatever the length of time involved may be, self-discipline requires the ability to think in terms of the future. Some people are all right so long as their future-oriented thinking is confined to the next hour. A smaller number are able to think in terms of tomorrow. Very few think much beyond that point.

The further into the future a person can project the consequences of his actions (or of his failure to take action), the more self-disciplined he is likely to be. For example, the person who is able to think in terms of five years from today is unlikely to live beyond his means. He will have the self-discipline to ignore the false prosperity of those around him and learn to live *beneath his means*. Ultimately, when the government's false-prosperity schemes go to their final resting place in Ponzi Heaven, his neighbors will, of course, be envious of him for having been prudent. But I'd rather be hated and financially stable than loved and standing in breadlines with imprudent neighbors.

Future-oriented thinking catalyzes the process of investing time, energy, pain, and sacrifice in tomorrow's rewards. Once again, exercise serves as a good illustration. It takes future-oriented thinking to be a disciplined jogger. You don't jog because it feels good; you don't jog because you like to socialize; you jog because you're convinced of the future benefits—particularly the cardiovascular benefits—tomorrow, next week, next year. There is overwhelming medical evidence that jogging improves the blood-pumping capacity of the heart, improves the body's capacity to process oxygen, and reduces blood pressure. If you're inclined to believe this evidence, and can relate it to the future, you will also be inclined to be a self-disciplined jogger. It's true that jogging is very time consuming—but, then, so is dying.

A future-oriented thinker is likely to exercise; an immediate-benefit thinker is likely to munch on a box of chocolates. A future-oriented thinker is likely to spend a great deal of time reading serious books; an immediate-benefit thinker is likely to spend a great deal of time watching sitcoms on television. A future-oriented thinker is likely to emphasize work; an immediate-benefit thinker is likely to emphasize play. If you're a future-oriented thinker, the likelihood is that you already lead a generally self-disciplined life. As a result, when tomorrow becomes today (as it does every day), you're likely to have far fewer problems to deal with than the average person.

CONSISTENCY

A self-disciplined individual not only understands the price of success and thinks of tomorrow's consequences, but he is *consistent* in his actions. He is consistent because he *concentrates* on being consistent. He continually chooses the right action over the instinctive action, and ultimately this consistency becomes an unconscious habit.

One of the reasons consistency is so important is that timing and circumstances play such a major role in the success or failure of any given objective, project, or venture. The most omniscient among us can, at best, make only educated guesses about when the timing and circumstances will be right for us, given the fact that Murphy* is always lurking in the shadows. But if we're consistent, we will be ready when the timing and circumstances do come together.

Ted Williams once said that in the course of a ball game a batter can expect to see a perfect pitch only once, so he has to be prepared every second that he's at the plate. I believe an analogy to this can be drawn for most aspects of life. It's only a matter of

---

*Murphy, as I use him throughout this book, is the personification of Murphy's Law, which states, in substance, that if anything *can* go wrong, it *will*.

time until everything is situated just right for you, and, when it is, *you* must be situated just right. And you will be if your actions have been consistent.

Al Davis, the charismatic owner of the Los Angeles Raiders, reflected on this point after the Raiders won the 1977 Super Bowl. For years the Raiders had posted the best record in football, but they had never made it to the Super Bowl, let alone won it. Davis pointed out that it wasn't a matter of not being able to win the big ones, but that football, as the saying goes, is a game of funny bounces. In addition, he pointed to the obvious fact that there are always many good teams competing for the title. The secret, Davis said, is to be *consistently good*, to stay near the top of the pack every year, and sooner or later your time will come. Sooner or later, everything will bounce right for you, and, when it does, *you* must be ready.

The archenemy of consistency is the exception. The most undisciplined people I have known lead exception-filled lives. There is always a special party to go to, a special game to see, a special event that's taking place. One such person I know, Barney Baffled, leads a totally frustrating life so cluttered with "exceptions" and "emergencies" that he can never quite pull it all together. Notwithstanding his enormous talents, he just can't seem to get out of the starting gate. He always has a "special problem"—a reason why today he cannot do the right thing instead of the instinctive thing. Tomorrow, of course, he will be self-disciplined; tomorrow everything will be fine. But *today* he has a "problem."

What Barney Baffled doesn't understand is the *Exception Theory:* He who makes an exception runs the risk of making a rule, because *exceptions tend to become rules.* One exception has a habit of leading to another, until life itself becomes one big exception.

Exceptions are *not* nonrecurring, as inconsistent people would like to believe. Exceptions may change form, but they continually appear. The only way to protect yourself from a life of exceptions is to live by the rule of *no exceptions.* This takes a great deal of character, because there will always be someone around who will try to intimidate you into making an exception—"just this once." You know, "Come on, just this one time isn't going to matter. Don't make such a big deal out of it. It's not going to kill you to miss one day." It's at *that* moment that your character is on the line. In such a situation, do *you* have the courage to say no?

Obviously, I realize that no one can or should go through life like an automaton, always walking the straight and narrow path. But the idea is to *strive* for perfection. By so doing, you might achieve an 85% or 90% self-discipline rating, whereas the person who doesn't even try will continue to live an exception-filled life that never seems to lead anywhere but to the next exception.

A long-ago discussion I had with my comedy-writing pal, Chubby Chuckle, probably made the biggest impact on me regarding the no-exceptions rule. In one of those rare serious moments, he told me how the woman he had been in love with for many years had died a slow, painful death of cancer. In somber detail he related what his ongoing torment had been like, right down to the day of her funeral. Obviously, his day-to-day life had been profoundly altered from the moment he had first realized he was going to lose her.

I asked Chubby how in the world he had been able to go on writing comedy material day after day with such a grievous problem on his mind; I never forgot his answer. He said, "I do it because it's my job. A bricklayer doesn't stop laying bricks when there's an illness in his family. I happen to write jokes for a living. Sure I was in constant pain, but I still had a job to do."

That was heavy stuff. Imagine writing jokes when you're crying inside. I was overwhelmed by the thought of the pain Chubby Chuckle must have experienced. Since that conversation, I've always figured that my problems are small by comparison, and rarely do I see them as deserving the status of exceptions. I constantly remind myself that it *doesn't matter* whether I'm "down," or tired, or not feeling too well, or just in a nonworking mood. To make certain that this point did not escape me, before I began writing my last book I authored the following prose and hung it on my wall:

I AM THE MACHINE

I labor the same number of hours, I put forth the same intensity, I tap the same creative powers, and I produce the same quality of work, without regard to circumstances of any kind.

Sickness is not a factor; being tired is irrelevant; all problems are aside and apart from the work that I, The Machine, do.

Because of the self-discipline and regimentation required of me, I have the willpower to avoid being distracted by anybody or anything that does not directly contribute to my project.

No person, activity, or situation can affect the relentless performance of me, The Machine.

I read this sign each morning before commencing to write. Whenever I started to feel a little "sick," or tired, or sorry for myself, I would read it again. It was like having a watchdog to keep me in line.

Without fail, I went to bed every evening between 9:00 and 9:30 P.M. If there was a "once in a lifetime" special on television, my lifetime just had to do without it. I arose each morning between 5:00 and 5:30 A.M., did my exercises, jogged four miles, showered, dressed, and proceeded to my writing quarters. The door to my writing room was always *dead-bolted*. No one was allowed inside—for *any* reason short of an emergency. Once disturbed, the first task of the person interrupting me was to convince me that the reason for the disruption deserved to be classified as an emergency.

I did not take phone calls (friends and business associates were told that I was in a writing session). I participated in no meetings (once again, unless the meeting could be classified as an emergency). I took lunch at my writing table, while continuing to write. I wrote when I was tired; I wrote when I didn't feel well; I wrote when I was uninspired (the writer's favorite excuse for not writing). There were no exceptions to speak of.

Sounds like a tough life, doesn't it? Well, all I can tell you is that heeding the Exception Theory and thinking about the future consequences of my actions has produced results. And just because I don't "play now and pay later" doesn't mean that I don't play. On the contrary, the fact that I do like to play is one of the very things that motivates me to be self-disciplined; I want to be able to *afford to play*. So I *pay now* and *play later*.

Consistency, like all other aspects of self-discipline, is crucial to matters of health—diet, sleep, nonsmoking, and nondrinking, to name but a few examples. Let's look at jogging one last time as a case in point. Every jogger knows that you don't always feel like jogging, future benefits notwithstanding. When I first began to jog, I often "postponed" my early morning run until that evening, because I "didn't feel up to it." Voilà—an amazing thing happened! More often than not, a "problem" would arise that would also prevent my jogging in the evening. And all too often that problem was simply that I still "didn't feel up to it." After several of these postponements-turned-cancellations, I began to realize that I would either have to heed the Exception Theory or forget about jogging. I decided to heed.

Likewise, I have observed firsthand that postponements are an integral part of the business world. It's not uncommon for a person's excuse for not producing results to be no more than the fact that he "just didn't feel up to it today." Tomorrow his situation will be better; then, of course, he will take care of the matter. Unfortunately, most people are like Barney Baffled and "tomorrow" never seems to come. Or, when it finally does arrive, it's far too late.

To be consistent, you must make a personal commitment to work *whether or not you feel like it*. If you're not inspired today, the safest assumption is that you won't be inspired tomorrow, either. Do it now!

Another serious stumbling block to consistency is what I refer to as the Obesity Creed, which states: "I've already blown it today, so I may as well enjoy myself." The last time I engaged in this dangerous rationalization, they almost had to haul me away from the restaurant on a flatbed truck. I refer to the episode nostalgically as The Battle of Little Big Pie.

It began innocently enough with a trip to Palm Springs. The previous week, my weight had been slowly creeping up. I was a little concerned, but not overly worried, because I had always been able to gain control of myself just before going over the edge of the Fat Pit. But in Palm Springs, I got a little rambunctious. I even took up a new hobby—nibbling. Candy, potato chips, tree bark, index cards—anything that fell into my path. As I waddled down the streets of Palm Springs, looking like The Thing, the locals began to panic. People screamed as I approached. I began to feel unwanted, unloved. But little did I know that I hadn't even scratched the surface of my caloric potential. My true championship form was not to show itself until Saturday, when I had dinner with my friend, Bulldog Drummer, the head of a large publishing house in New York.

As I sat in the restaurant Saturday evening, panting and sweating, Bulldog tactfully mentioned to me that it looked as though I had "put on a little weight." I suspected that his remark had been prompted by the fact that I had eaten all the bread on the table and had started to butter my left forefinger. Finally, I came right out with it: "I don't know how this got started, but lately I've been eating like a wild boar. Anyway, I've already gone so far over the line that nothing else I eat tonight will make much difference anyway. This is already a lost weekend, so I may as well go all the way."

That was the go-ahead signal! You could hear the trumpets blaring in the background as I mounted a ground offensive against the kitchen. Bulldog and his wife trembled in awe, expressing fear and disbelief when at last I ordered dessert. The piece of coconut cream pie that the waiter brought out must have been the largest portion ever served to a mammal west of the Rockies. I got the distinct feeling that he was mocking me.

I still remember Bulldog asking me, incredulously, "Are you going to eat that *whole thing?*" I was already totally disgusted with myself, so why not go for it. What difference would another few thousand calories make? I must immodestly tell you that it was an incredible finish, right out of the movie "Fatso." Everyone in the restaurant who had thrilled to the sight of Dom DeLuise and his pals chanting in unison, "Get the honey," couldn't help but feel a twinge of excitement as my head fell forward into my plate. I had done it. I had gone the distance with that gargantuan piece of pie.

When I awoke the next morning with a hangover, I realized that it was either back to the law of no exceptions or back to the way things had been many years before, when I had lived by the philosophy of the Obesity Creed. The decision wasn't hard to make. One glance at an old picture of myself was all it took. In that worn and crumpled photo, I looked like an experiment gone wrong—a corpulent cross between Wimpy and Sidney Green-street. And why not? In the old days I had set world records in freestyle watermelon eating, brownie receptions, and the wind-aided buttered-popcorn dash. I competed professionally under the name of Tubby Tortoise. My daily excuse was that I had already blown it for *that* day, so I may as well go all the way. And I darn near went all the way—to my grave.

What finally turned me around was future thinking and the two keys to consistency—the Exception Theory and the Salvage Theory, the latter being the converse of the Obesity Creed. The *Salvage Theory* states: On bad days, instead of taking the attitude that you may as well eat all you want because you've already blown it, cut your losses short and *salvage the day*. Just because you gorged yourself at lunch doesn't mean you need to gorge yourself at dinner. Catch yourself before you go from bad to worse. Contrary to the beliefs of those who live by the Obesity Creed, one more bite *does* hurt. No matter how much you've already eaten, eating more certainly is not going to help. But it *will* make matters worse.

Heeding the Salvage Theory will serve you well in all areas of life. Just because you didn't jog today doesn't mean you shouldn't do your sit-ups. Just because you had a bad morning at the office doesn't mean you shouldn't dig in and get something accomplished this afternoon. Just because you had a fight with your lover earlier in the evening doesn't mean you should compound the problem by purposely trying to start another one now. Learn the art of salvaging bad days. Be consistent. Anyone can do well on good days; only successful people know how to make headway on the bad ones.

One last roadblock to consistency that I should mention is sort of an adjunct to the Obesity Creed—the New Year's Resolution Hoax. All too often, the next thing out of the mouth of the person who rationalizes away today is, "I'm going to start my diet Monday," or "I'm going to start making ten sales calls a day, without fail, beginning the first of the month," or "I'm going to start jogging religiously January 1st," or "I'm going to start studying next quarter." The empirical evidence overwhelmingly suggests that the New Year's Resolution Hoax *does not work.* In fact, it suggests that it's a—well, a hoax—a self-perpetrated hoax.

The time to start a diet is *today.* The time to start working is *today.* The time to start exercising is *today.* The time to start studying is *today.* Otherwise, making resolutions becomes little more than a game, and the consistent, self-disciplined person does not play games with important aspects of his life. He does not come bolting out of the starting gate on January 1, only to fade badly when February arrives, then drop completely out of the race by March. Rather, he moves briskly, but calmly, away from the starting gate *today,* and continues at a steady, controlled pace *for the rest of his life.* He does not "diet"; he stays slim as a way of life. (Obviously, the latter statement is metaphorical with regard to *all* aspects of life.)

The self-discipline rules I have discussed thus far have dramatically changed my life over the past ten years, and I expect them to be even more valuable to me in the future as those about me are losing their heads (figuratively speaking, I hope). Best of all, they are responsible for lifting me from perennial contender

"My lord, he's done it. What stamina!"

for the Fatty Arbuckle Award to the title of Mr. Reptile America.
Eat your heart out, Arnold.

DETERMINATION

Determination is the father of perseverance, which is the ultimate
test of self-discipline. A determined individual is a persistent individual. Such an individual will persevere despite obstacles, hard-
ships, bad luck, opposition, or discouragement. Obviously,
determination is not a quality exhibited by today's average Western man. One stubbed toe and he goes whining to the government
for help.

This pervasive crybaby attitude in our society is both a curse
and a blessing. It most certainly is a curse to Western Civilization, because a civilization consists of people. When people are
not determined, their civilization is not determined. When people
do not persevere, their civilization does not persevere.

But it's also a blessing—for you. We've already established
that the one piece of good news in the otherwise discouraging age
in which we live is that, because people have been encouraged to
be lazy, ignorant, and incompetent, you can expect to have very
little competition if you're one of the few who chooses to stand
right side up. Likewise, because most people have neither the
courage nor the inclination to fight the good fight *to the finish*,
the determined individual has the field pretty much to himself.

The man who is determined understands well the meaning of
the words of the seventeenth-century Spanish Jesuit, Baltasar
Gracián, who said simply and profoundly: "Time and I against
any other two." There is no partner so powerful as time. If one
does his part by remaining determined and consistent despite
obstacles and disappointments, time will take care of the rest.
The story of today's hard-luck kid becoming tomorrow's hero has
been duplicated tens of thousands of times throughout history.
But the formula works only if you keep *your* end of the bargain—
only if you are determined to hang in there until time comes to
the rescue and works its wonders.

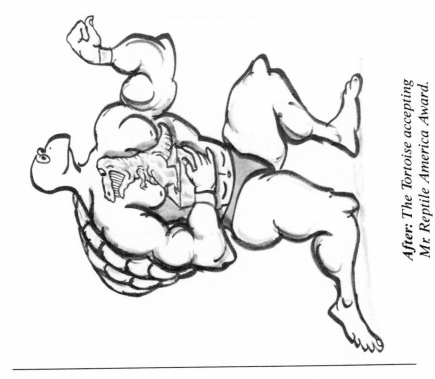

After: The Tortoise accepting Mr. Reptile America Award.

Before: The Tortoise accepting Fatty Arbuckle Award.

To be determined, you must want something badly enough to endure the pain necessary to obtain it. Ironically, one of the things that causes many people to lose their drive is *success itself*. Success often causes people to fall into what Charles A. Garfield, president of Peak Performance Center in Berkeley, California, calls the "comfort zone."

This problem was the central theme of the movie, "Rocky III." People who have lapsed into the comfort zone have lost what ex-champ Apollo Creed referred to as the "eye of the tiger." Rocky Balboa may be a fictional character, but his story is lived every day in the real world. After three years as champion, he lapsed into the comfort zone and had the misfortune of running into the likes of Clubber Lang. Following an unmerciful beating at the hands of the indelicate Mr. Lang, Rocky commenced to wallow in self-pity. He lacked the motivation to win back his title. He no longer had that determined look in his eye—the look he had sported years earlier when he had relentlessly stalked Apollo Creed. He had lost the *eye of the tiger*. And, like people in real life who have lost their determination, he had lost something else along with it—his happiness.

This true-to-life story had a great impact on me, because I immediately connected it with Viktor Frankl's observation that what man needs is an objective to strive for rather than a tensionless state. Having personally experienced the same phenomenon, I am convinced that only a corpse can be at peace in a tensionless state. At the point in my life when I had lost my focus and lapsed into the comfort zone, I became bored, disenchanted, and unhappy. I finally realized that something was missing from my life—the simple pleasure of striving, the excitement of working toward an objective.

The determined man possesses an inexorable drive, a Joblike tenacity that pushes him on against all obstacles. Without this drive, success is not possible, because obstacles are a fact of life. Sometimes the obstacles become so great that you begin to wonder if the Man upstairs might not be punishing you for some long-forgotten immoral act you may have committed.

Black Bart once said that "no one is protected from the Triple Bypass—bad luck, bad timing, and bad product." But Nietzsche said, "That which does not kill me, makes me stronger." Both of them being legendary philosophers, it is not surprising that they're both right. No human being can stand up to the Triple Bypass, but he *can* gain strength from the experience and rise up again. Black Bart likes to point to his partner, Sundance Sid, as an ideal example.

He says that Sundance, back in the early seventies, went from a net worth of $600 million one day to minus $6 million the next, when his multibillion-dollar corporation almost went under. According to Black Bart, Sundance, without flinching, just "picked himself up, brushed himself off, and kept right on going." In view of this, it's of more than just passing interest that he was a partner in Black Bart's Louisiana gas-drilling deal. It's also worth noting that, in between, Sundance was floored by the Triple Bypass on at least one other occasion that I am aware of.

Another great story of determination is that of Jose Maria Ruiz Mateos, reputed to be the richest man in Spain (prior to the nationalization of his businesses by the Spanish government in February 1983.) Back in 1958, when Señor Mateos was just getting started, his big "break" came when he succeeded in obtaining an exclusive contract to supply sherry to John Harvey & Sons Ltd. of England. The quotation marks around the word *break* are for good reason. Sr. Mateos had to write *thirty-three* letters just to get an interview at John Harvey! It's not surprising that the emblem of his company, Rumasa, is a busy worker bee. It may now appear to the average person that everything Sr. Mateos touches turns to gold, but how many of those people would have been persistent enough to write even two or three letters—let alone *thirty-three*—in an effort to get their foot in the door?

It's important for people who aspire to success to hear true stories like these so they do not, as we discussed in Chapter 4, hold false perceptions of what it takes to succeed. *All* successful people overcome major obstacles, so don't make the mistake of thinking that your obstacles are unique. They're not.

"I dunno, Bart, he looks awfully scared to me. Maybe he's not in good enough shape to undergo a Triple Bypass."

It's not that life is *full* of problems; life *is* problems. Rather than be surprised each time you encounter an obstacle, it's far healthier to view life as one endless series of problems. If you use that as your starting point—the given—then it's obvious that to the extent you're able to cope with problems, you will be happy and successful; to the extent that you're unable to cope with problems, you will be unhappy and unsuccessful. Since problems are continual, the only variable is how one deals with them.

Rule number one for handling problems is to refrain from panicking. When a bad situation develops, go to a quiet place and calmly review the matter. Identify and analyze the mistakes you've made so you can avoid making the same ones in the future. Then, instead of complaining about your bad luck, immediately begin to think of ways to *maximize* the situation—i.e., to make the most of it. I cannot recall a failure I have experienced, no matter how painful, that did not give birth to something positive.

Whenever I follow this procedure, I usually end up getting angry with *myself*. Even if I believe that someone else has caused my problem, I try to focus on what *I* should have done to protect myself against his actions. I learned long ago that the corner grocer won't accept excuses in exchange for a pound of hamburger. That is not to say that there's not a *reason* for failure, but there's a difference between a "reason" and an "excuse." A reason *explains* the failure, and there's always an explanation for failure. But an excuse implies clemency. And, in the real world, the people who sell you products and services aren't into clemency. They're into money. An excuse has no intrinsic value.

Overeating because you were at a party last night may be a *reason* why you put on weight, but it's no *excuse*; you still end up with the extra weight. Not studying may be a *reason* why you flunked a course, but it's no *excuse*; you still have to take the course over again. Listening to an unknowledgeable stockbroker may be a *reason* why you lost your money, but it's no *excuse*; you still don't have the money to spend on other things.

In the words of Napoleon Hill: "Success requires no explanations. Failure permits no alibis." The man with determination understands this point very well, so instead of concentrating on excuses, he concentrates on overcoming obstacles; he persists in the face of seemingly impossible odds. If you study such a man closely, the look you see is unmistakable—it's the *eye of the tiger*. And when his determination leads to victory, as it ultimately does, you also see a happy, successful person.

SECTION
III

LOSERS TALK;
WINNERS ACT

CHAPTER VII

On the
Plains of Hesitation

If we can learn anything at all from government, it's that the absence of long-term planning leads to certain disaster. The empirical evidence suggests that government's long-term planning efforts fall into three categories: 1) nonexistent; 2) erratic; 3) based on false premises. William Simon, former Secretary of the Treasury, disrobes the truth about government planning this way:

> One of the things I learned during my tenure in Washington is that the civics book picture of government in operation is completely inaccurate. The idea that our elected officials take part in a careful decision-making process—monitoring events, reviewing options, responsibly selecting policies—has almost no connection with reality. A more accurate image would be that of a runaway train with the throttle stuck wide open—while the passengers and crew are living it up in the dining car.

As in so many other areas of our lives, government sets the example. Expediency is everything; the long term does not exist. The immediate benefit is all that counts. Eat, drink, and be merry, for tomorrow Lee Iacocca or Bozo the Clown may be president.

Like their democratic rulers, most people live from day to day, even hour to hour. They have no master plan for the future, no strategy to follow. Like the government, they have become in-ured to crises. They simply deal with problems as they arise, and, as a result, their solutions are almost always ineffective.

It's unlikely that you would get in your car and begin a long, important journey without a road map. Yet most people do the equivalent of just that every day of their lives. They have abso-lutely no idea how they intend to reach their long-term objec-tives—if indeed they even have such objectives. The journey through life is the longest and most important trip you'll ever take, so it deserves the clearest and most accurate road map pos-sible. That road map is your own long-term planning, which, if properly devised, should comprise a detailed strategy for reaching your future goals.

At best, the objective of long-term planning is to avoid crises. At the very least, it is to be prepared, far in advance, to handle such crises as quickly and inexpensively as possible when they do arise.

The long term has a persistent habit of becoming the present rather quickly, which seems continually to amaze people. Don't make the mistake of thinking of the long term as some vague point in time so far into the future that it will never actually make its appearance. It will, and almost always sooner than you antici-pate. Since most people in the Western world are guilty of making this mistake, it puts you at a decided advantage if you are one of the few who takes the trouble to lay out a detailed, realistic strat-egy for the future, *based on a sound perception of the world around you.*

Long-term planning, by its very nature, is at odds with pro-crastination. It does you little good to lay out a battle plan once the missile is out of the silo. Every day that you put off organizing your plans brings the future one day closer to the present. It's hard work, maybe the hardest thing you'll ever do, but, remem-ber, we're talking about the happiness and success of the only life you will ever have.

Ironically, many people who seem to understand the perilous state of Western Civilization often seem to be ill-prepared to face the future consequences of its demise. The reason for this can often be traced to fear. Sometimes a person's knowledge of the facts makes him so fearful of tomorrow that mental paralysis sets in. He does not understand that, regardless of what the future holds, life *will* go on.

A person who in 1945 could have envisioned the social and economic environment of today would have made a grave mistake had he concluded that there was no sense in planning for the future. While the Western world of the 1980's, compared to that of the 1940's, may seem like one massive slave state, the fact remains that those who planned ahead, and followed through on those plans, have enjoyed an abundance of happiness and prosperity during the past forty years. Life *has* gone on.

Life has always been tough. So what's new? Those who panic fall by the wayside. Those who keep their heads, who keep calm and continue to move forward within the boundaries of a specific strategy, endure and prosper. That's what survival of the fittest is all about.

It is not mental paralysis, however, that immobilizes the majority of people. Most people fail to take action on the grounds that "the timing never seems to be quite right." Murphy said that if anything can go wrong, it will, at the worst possible moment. A corollary to this is the *Timing Theory:* Conditions are never right at the right time; the timing is *always* wrong! If you are waiting for everything to be just right before taking action, you are in possession of a foolproof excuse for failure. The fact is that you can always find a reason for not doing something, and the most convenient reason of all is that "the timing just isn't quite right."

The truth of the matter is that, in the final analysis, whether or not you take action will depend upon how much you really want something. If you desire happiness and financial success badly enough in the years ahead, you'll stop making excuses and start making plans. All the knowledge in the world is useless without action.

People are fond of saying that if they had it to do over again, they would do it differently, but now, of course, it's "too late." The antidote for this excuse, to paraphrase Viktor Frankl, is to pretend as though you were *already* living for the second time, with the knowledge that your excuse for procrastinating the first time was that the conditions were never quite right. The conditions will *never* be "right," and you will *always* feel as though it's "too late." The important thing is to apply the Salvage Theory: Get started now, no matter what the problems are and no matter how long you've already procrastinated.

If not, well—as an unknown author once said: "On the plains of hesitation bleach the bones of countless millions who, on the verge of victory, sat down to rest, and, while resting, died."

It's a good time to remind ourselves of the three important questions posed in Chapter 3:

1. What do I want out of life?
2. What will it cost me (in terms of time, energy, pain, and sacrifice)?
3. Am I willing to pay the necessary price?

We've already discussed some of the costs: the necessity of developing the ability and courage to make accurate perceptions, of avoiding contact with dishonest people and constantly scrutinizing your own actions, and of faithfully practicing self-discipline and perseverance. However, while each of these is crucial to success, none of them directly prods you to answer the first question—What do I want out of life?

Mapping a strategy for the future, however, virtually forces you to think this question through carefully. Otherwise, planning becomes a meaningless exercise. In addition, once you see what's involved in laying out a realistic plan and taking specific action on that plan (the cost), you will undoubtedly want to devote some hard thinking to whether or not you are willing to pay the necessary price, or at least how much of it you're willing to pay.

These questions are inextricably tied to one another. After all, each of us has an infinite number of desires, so, standing alone, the question of what you want out of life is not really meaningful. Limits are placed on your desires by the price tags attached to them and by your willingness and ability to pay those prices. This is where an accurate perception of the realities of today's world is crucial. The time, energy, pain, and sacrifice needed to surmount the obstacles of today are quite different in degree and scope from the time, energy, pain, and sacrifice that were required even ten or twenty years ago.

Long-term planning involves decision making, and, as I pointed out, if your perceptions are inaccurate, you're bound to make wrong decisions. It is not a good idea to ignore Nature's most basic law. First, foremost, and always: *Actions have consequences.* The consequences of faulty long-term planning can be not only disastrous, but irreversible. And if you harbor erroneous perceptions of the world around you, you are *guaranteeing* that your plans will be flawed.

That's why it's so important for you to have an accurate perception of the moral revolution that has taken place in the Western world, as well as the ongoing collapse of its economic and social structure. Such a perception gives you a considerable advantage over most of your friends, neighbors, and business associates, very few of whom would even consider thinking in such uncomfortable and unfamiliar terms.

But even if you're fully aware of the moral revolution that has taken place in our society, and of the accelerating social changes now in progress, you still must come to grips with what that really means. Just to say that Western Civilization is collapsing is inane. The actions of a shameless, immoral government and a desperate, anything-goes populace have *specific* consequences.

These consequences are obvious to any rational, *intellectually honest* individual—which, of course, eliminates a majority of the current population. However much one may dislike hearing it, coming to grips with the meaning of the collapse of Western Civilization means coming to grips with the fact that most of the things you've been reading about for years in so-called gloom-and-doom books—books that have been glibly dismissed by the media—are *true.* As day follows night, there are predictable consequences to the economic and sociopolitical actions that spring from a desires-are-rights society. In reality, the doom-and-gloom books have done little more than point to many of these very obvious consequences.

Yes, the United States, and probably all Western nations, *will* default on their national debts.

Yes, many major corporations, and possibly whole industries, *will* be nationalized.

Yes, there *will* be runaway inflation, even if it is preceded by a deflationary depression.

Yes, the president *will* impose price controls (in the real world, there is no such thing as "wage controls"), and widespread shortages *will* result.

Yes, as a result of shortages, black markets *will* comprise a substantial portion of the national economy.

Yes, Social Security *will* either be declared bankrupt or be paid off in worthless dollars.

Yes, you *will* be barred from moving capital out of the country.

Yes, interest rates *will* ultimately soar to 50%, 100%, and beyond.

Yes, there *will* be rioting and bloodshed in major cities, on a scale never before dreamed of.

Yes, martial law *will* be imposed.

This is only a small sampling of the consequences that can no longer be avoided, short of Divine intervention. In the years ahead, count on more greed, more guilt, more dishonesty, and, above all, more envy. Envy is the fuel of political fires, and its supply appears to be unlimited. As a result, count on a continuation of the trend toward punishing winners and rewarding losers. Count on its accelerating.

Psychologically facing up to these kinds of consequences may be the most difficult hurdle for you to clear in the pursuit of a better life for you and your family in the years ahead. Because you've been assured by the Galbraithians for so long that this kind of talk is sheer nonsense, such notions may not be able to penetrate your mental paradigm. However, it may help to remember that these Galbraithians are the same intimidators who for years told you that banks and savings and loans were in fine shape, who laughed when "doom and gloomers" suggested that many of America's largest corporations were headed for disaster, who insisted that an inflation rate in excess of 8% was unthinkable, who smirked and shook their heads patronizingly when many hard-money newsletter writers predicted interest rates in excess of 20%, and who assured everyone that financial chaos was now impossible because of government controls (which, of course, are the very cause of the financial chaos in the first place).

The majority of fiscal conservatives and free-market advocates were blinded by the glare of false hopes when Ronald Reagan took office. They naively believed that President Reagan's victory demonstrated a shift in people's attitudes toward a cutback in both government benefits and the size of government.

Unfortunately, they completely missed the point of the election. What most Reagan voters really were saying was, "All I know is that I'm a lot worse off than before that idiot Carter took office. I don't understand supply-side economics, or any other kind of economics—*and I don't want to understand.* I just want my free slice of pie—make that pie *à la mode*—and I want it *now.* So I'm willing to give Reagan a chance to prove that his program can work—work for *me,* that is! If he can deliver more goodies within a reasonable period of time, fine; if not, bring on the next guy. But don't bother me with economics, ideology, morality, or any other intellectual chatter."

Not one voter in a thousand understood that the collapse of Western Civilization had already entered its latter stages before Ronald Reagan even took office. The course of destruction was set long ago by the political criminals who originally implemented the myriad of government theft programs now in place. The kamikaze mission of fiscal suicide has been on automatic pilot for years and is now rapidly heading toward its final destination.

Of course, the tens of millions of people addicted to these "benefits" ignorantly believe that the kamikaze plane is going to experience a smooth landing in some tropical paradise filled with more homes, more automobiles, more television sets, and plenty of cotton candy. In reality, however, the plane is nose-diving into a sea of inflation!

If you still have a mental block when it comes to getting by this all-important psychological step, then I recommend a thorough examination of the facts. *Hard study* would be even more prudent. A preponderance of evidence can often break down the psychological barriers for an intelligent, rational individual.

There is nothing wrong with hoping, even praying, for a miracle to occur, provided that's not the only step you plan to take. If, indeed, a supernatural force puts our widespread disease into a state of remission, you can be sure that I'll be right in there with you celebrating the good news. But I certainly would not be so foolish as to plan my life around the assumption that such a miracle will take place. When the home team is twenty-one points down in the last quarter, a person might display great loyalty by continuing to root for victory; on the other hand, he would display great stupidity if he allowed his emotions to motivate him to place a bet on the team at that late stage of the game.

The word *survival* has been bandied about so irreverently by the media that it automatically conjures up images of crazies practicing bayonet training in the wilderness. Most people consider so-called survival talk nonsense. In reality, however, it would not be just imprudent, but absurd, for a person *not* to be concerned with his own survival and the survival of his family.

When I speak of survival, I am speaking, first of all, of staying alive and healthy. Second, I am speaking of making yourself and your family as comfortable as possible under whatever circumstances you encounter. More specifically, I'm talking about food, clothing, shelter, and self-defense, and, on a secondary level, discretionary comforts. I see nothing particularly abnormal about such objectives, contrary to media putdowns.

Ironically, the millions of people who cavalierly toss aside "survival talk" as nonsense are, without consciously thinking about it, striving toward these exact same objectives. Everyone unconsciously strives to stay alive and enhance his well-being. It's just that most people never give staying alive a second thought, and they assume that government benevolence assures their well-being. (Poor souls.)

My advice in the remaining chapters of this section is based on my perception of the consequences of government's and voters' actions—past, present, and future. It is not my objective here to give you specific instructions on how to build a hideaway, grow food, or operate a generator. My intention is to give you an overview of certain areas that I feel should be an integral part of your long-term planning, and thus stimulate you to begin to think seriously about them.

I use the term *overview*, because I believe it would be presumptuous of me to attempt to write in depth about topics that require highly specialized knowledge. By giving you an overview, I hope to point you in the *right direction*, because if you're headed down the wrong road, you will never arrive at your long-term objectives, no matter how profound your understanding.

And pointing you in the right direction is a matter of helping you to recognize what it is that you're going to have to cope with in the years ahead. With regard to that, I am now going to make the following three guarantees about the future (I emphasize that these are not projections, but *guarantees*):

1. There will be a complete destruction of the currency of the United States, and probably that of every other Western nation.

2. There will be severe shortages of the "necessities" of life.

3. As a result of the first two, there will be civil disorder and violence of a magnitude never before seen in America.

If I'm right about the above, then your survival—your ability to acquire and safeguard sufficient food, clothing, shelter, and discretionary comforts, as well as your ability to defend yourself and your family—will depend upon how well you understand the consequences of these guarantees and what actions you take to counteract such consequences. In the next three chapters, I will examine these consequences and discuss my ideas on how best to deal with them.

CHAPTER VIII

A Friendly Little Game of Old Maid

We have already discussed the unavoidable economic consequences of a desires-are-rights society. On a more personal level, however, consider the following: To find out how much you are making in terms of 1940 dollars, just subtract approximately 95% of your current income. *That* is the economic consequence that most concerns *you*. And it's only going to get worse.

Contrary to Ronald Reagan's tough talk, and contrary to daily media reports about how the plight of "the poor" has worsened under his administration, the fact is that there have been *no meaningful cutbacks in federal handouts* since Reagan took office. Quite the opposite, in fact: today the federal deficit is expanding almost exponentially. Never—not even once—has any liberal economist, politician, or media expert suggested how this deficit problem is ultimately to be resolved. Short of some new welfare-state "miracle," the federal government will have no choice but to stick with the old reliable pseudo-miracle of creating money out of thin air—via the Bureau of Engraving and Printing.

There's only one problem with this "solution": The "money" that comes rolling off the presses isn't really money at all. It's only paper, which creates yet another problem: As more and more people begin to figure this out, they want more and more of the paper—in the form of higher prices—to compensate for its lack of value. Which leads to the ultimate problem: People finally figure out that the paper really has *no* value. And that's when they refuse to accept it *at all* in exchange for their goods and services. It is at that point that the currency, with the swiftness of a wastebasket full of paper going up in flames, rushes to its deserving demise.

Of course, different people catch on to the paper-money scheme at different times and to different degrees, and each person reacts in different ways. And if a person reacts too late—well, he who hesitates always has the option of repapering his living room in a nice, gray/green color. Some pundits have likened it to a game of Old Maid: Whoever ends up with the Old Maid (paper currency) has, in effect, given away his products and labor for nothing. If you don't believe this, just ask the millions of people who have already given theirs away in the numerous countries that have experienced runaway inflation.

Though the subtle destruction of paper currency is taking place daily, the official burial is probably still several years off. I honestly cannot say whether that will be in three or four years, or ten or twelve years, because there are far too many unknowns to be certain. One of the *knowns,* however, is that the government, through the use of force, will continue to artificially repress the natural consequences of its debasement policy for as long as it is able—as it has been doing in this matter for decades. To its ultimate dismay, however, it will *not* be able to stave off the unpleasant consequences of its actions indefinitely. Therefore, the wise approach for you to take is to begin to abandon paper currency *now,* at a pace that is practical with your own living and business needs. This means exchanging paper for "hard assets," things that have intrinsic value (i.e., utility value).*

The most telltale indication that it's time to start getting se-

---

*John Pugsley has defined utility value as the value that people place on an object based on the use to which they put it, without regard to the value placed on it for investment or speculative purposes.

rious about shifting into hard assets is that the government and, of course, paper-money institutions have of late been dramatically exhorting the public to do the *opposite*. There has been a substantial increase in speeches and advertisements along these lines; people are being admonished to "save"—i.e., to hold on to their paper money by lending it to financial institutions. In point of fact, what the federal Big Liar and the financial industry are really doing is urging people to commit financial suicide.

In deciding what to convert your paper money into, while it can still be converted into something, your personal circumstances and objectives are of paramount importance. Depending upon these circumstances and objectives, you may either want to speculate with your capital, invest it, simply try to preserve it, or do a little of each. By *speculation*, I mean choosing to go into risky situations in the hopes of making large profits. By *investing*, I mean putting capital into ventures or instruments that you believe will bring you a "reasonable" return on your money. By *preservation*, I mean safeguarding your capital without regard to making a profit.

Obviously, the safest approach, *long term*, is to bet against government. Which means betting *on* political expediency. Which means betting on more and more government handouts. Which means betting on larger and larger deficits. Which means betting on government's printing more and more paper money. Which means betting on paper money's ultimately becoming worthless.

But be careful. Keep an eye out for changing conditions. Even though you may be right in your long-term analyses of various investments and speculations, you can go broke in the short run. As an example, it is possible (however remotely) that we could experience a temporary period of deflation prior to entering the homestretch of the politically inevitable runaway inflation. Therefore, no matter how certain you feel about the long term, unless you are prepared to tough it out until the truth rises up and takes control of the financial markets, you would be wise to proceed with the utmost caution.

With this caveat understood, I am going to break down the

alternatives for getting out of paper money, but the categories will not be speculation, investing, and preservation. Instead, I will categorize these alternatives in a way that more accurately reflects the realities of our brave new world.

CAPITAL BLACK HOLES

Much like the black holes of the far reaches of outer space, which ravenously suck in all matter that comes their way, there are black holes in the financial markets that can make capital vanish without a trace. Unlike their counterparts in interstellar space, however, Capital Black Holes can occasionally be persuaded to release their prey. Capital caught in a Capital Black Hole can escape, albeit injured, if its owner takes the proper action before it's too late. On the other hand, if the owner of capital trapped in a Capital Black Hole leaves it there in the hopes that it will eventually resurface on its own, he is ignorantly, stubbornly, and/or naively assuring that it will never be seen or heard from again.

Capital Black Holes include: certificates of deposit at either banks or savings and loans; cash-value life insurance (i.e., "whole life" or "ordinary life"); government, municipal, and corporate bonds; and long-term, fixed-rate mortgages or "deeds of trust." All of these pieces of paper are, in the words of Dr. Franz Pick, "certificates of guaranteed confiscation." You are absolutely *guaranteed* to lose virtually all of your capital, over the long pull, if you commit it to any of these Capital Black Holes.

In the short term, the process is reasonably painless, because you lose only a little of your capital each year. In fact, to the degree you are willing to delude yourself, you may feel no pain at all. The process is really quite simple: The fixed return paid by any of these Capital Black Hole debtors is not enough to compensate for taxes and price inflation. As a result, you *automatically* lose a portion of your capital each year. (While it is true that municipal bonds are presently tax free, price inflation alone during the coming years will be quite sufficient not only to offset any

"Wow! Look at 'em disappear."

interest paid on these bonds, but to chip away at the principal as well.) The sooner you rescue your capital from a Capital Black Hole, the better your capital's chances of making a full recovery.

In the long term, the pain is acute. Not only do taxes and price inflation eventually swallow virtually all of your capital, but a great many—perhaps even a majority—of the Capital Black Hole issuers will ultimately go bankrupt. I am speaking here of legal bankruptcy, as opposed to technical bankruptcy. A large percentage of these entities are already *technically* bankrupt.

Savings and Loans and Banks

To understand the illiquidity of the banking industry and the insolvency of a large segment of the savings and loan industry, one must look at these "institutions" for what they really are. (By *illiquidity*, I mean that current assets are less than current liabilities; by *insolvency* I mean that total assets are less than total liabilities.)

A bank or savings and loan is nothing more than a middleman, which is a somewhat dignified word for "broker." As a matter of fact, banks and savings and loans are really just glorified syndicators—the only syndicators, I might add, who do not have to file prospectuses with the Securities and Exchange Commission. They are free to solicit money from millions of investors, then turn right around and "invest" the large pools of money thereby generated in mortgages, stocks, bonds, and other "investment vehicles."

This cozy little exemption would be delightful, but for one problem. For years, these exempted syndicators have been borrowing money from depositors short term and lending (or "investing") it long term, sometimes for as long as thirty years. That means that *every* bank and *every* savings and loan is illiquid, aside and apart from the fact that many of them are insolvent. Their ability to repay their depositors' money is entirely dependent upon their success in raising additional money from new depositors. (This is commonly known as "pyramiding," but don't get any bright ideas. It's against the law for *you* to do it.)

"Step right up, fella, and deposit your money in a nice little 'risk-free' account."

Forget about "IRA accounts"; forget about "all-savers certificates"; forget about all the other gimmicks that these Capital
Black Hole issuers are frantically coming up with in a desperate
effort to keep from going under. All of these are nothing more
than attempts to disguise the bankrupt wolf as Little Red Riding
Hood's grandmother. In the years ahead, there are going to be
millions of people, minus their life's savings, who are going to be
just a bit irritated with certain entertainment figures who urged
them, via radio and television commercials, to put their money
into "risk-free" savings institutions. In fact, such ads collectively
constitute yet another of the biggest lies ever told—right up there
with today's accepted description of liberals.

Even if inflation does not completely wipe out the principal
in these "tax-free" accounts (which it will), count on the government, in a last-ditch effort to bail out its bankrupt programs, to
pass retroactive laws to tax all types of pension schemes previously declared to be tax free. Remember, the government has
the power to change the rules at will—and does! Pension funds
and various kinds of pension savings accounts are government
traps. They make it possible for the bureaucrats to know where
your assets are, which in turn makes it convenient for them to get
at those assets quickly (under the guise of an "emergency," of
course).

And, for goodness' sake, I hope by now you're well aware
that money deposited in banks and savings and loans is *not* in-
sured, in the true sense of the word. The assets of the Federal
Deposit Insurance Corporation and Federal Savings and Loan Insurance Corporation amount to only a tiny fraction of the trillions
of dollars that are deposited in banks and savings and loans, and,
to make matters worse, most of these assets are in the form of
very questionable government securities. (A recent study showed
that over 500 U.S. banks have more than 20% of their assets tied
up in New York City securities, while 179 maintain 50% or more
of their capital in these and New York State accounts.)

More recently, the savings-and-loan ads have been emphasiz-
ing that Congress has passed a resolution saying that the United

States government's "full faith and credit" stands behind every dollar deposited with them. First of all, if the depositors' money was safe, the government would not find it necessary to pass such a resolution. Second, the government is the *least* credit-worthy of *all* entities. If Washington ever has to make good on its "full faith and credit" (and you can count on its being called upon to do just that), you and I know very well where the "money" is going to have to come from—break out the extra-large paper rolls and haul in the fresh ink!

As the economic collapse continues to worsen, the problem is compounded. Not only do financial institutions have to borrow short, but they have to do so at rates that destroy any hope of turning a profit. Worse, they have to relend the money to questionable borrowers, because credit-worthy borrowers are reluctant to borrow at such high rates. Thus the interest-rate spiral accelerates onward and upward toward infinity.

Ultimately, there will probably be a "run" on banks and savings and loans, which in turn will force them to dump securities and mortgages at huge losses. It will then become a panic, and suddenly *everyone* will want to get his money out of these Capital Black Holes. Or, as Gary North puts it, "When a majority of depositors become convinced that a majority of depositors have become convinced that a majority of depositors are going to try to get their money out simultaneously, a majority of depositors start trying to get their money out simultaneously."

Insurance Companies

Insurance companies are not much better off. First, they have a majority of their assets tied up in bonds and mortgages, which is like the blind leading the blind. Second, as times get tougher, more and more people will want to borrow on the cash value of their life-insurance policies. This money is lent at rates far below the going interest rates in the financial markets, which, of course, is a disaster for the insurance companies. If too many people decide to borrow the amounts they are legally entitled to, then insurance companies, like banks, are forced to dump securities and mortgages at depressed market prices, which can lead to insolvency.

Government and Corporate Bonds

Government and corporate bonds, of course, are a joke among sophisticated investors. On the one hand, the federal government is a hopeless deadbeat, along with its state and municipal partners in crime. On the other hand, these bankrupt entities, in a continual effort to put out their own fires, continue to devastate corporations (and thus corporate bonds) through high taxes. Squeezed by these onerous taxes—along with price inflation, piranhalike trade unions, falling demand for their products, and consumer, health, and environmental regulations, among other problems—the balance sheets of most large corporations are looking more and more like they just came out of an alley fight with Bigfoot.

While it is true that whenever interest rates drop sufficiently short term (bond prices rise when interest rates decline), you might be able to make enough of a spread (through an increase in bond prices) to cover taxes and price inflation, it's pretty much wishful thinking. First, the long-term direction of interest rates is up—way up—and you would have to be a lot more omniscient than the so-called experts to catch so brief a downward trend before it bottoms out and starts moving in the other direction again. Second, it's doubtful that any such downward trend would be significant enough to bring bond prices up to a profitable level. So why bother to take the risk? Especially when you know that, even if you win, you will only be paid off in more paper. Besides, this book is concerned with long-term survival, not speculation.

Mortgages

The "entity" behind a mortgage, or deed of trust, is a piece of real estate, and the problems associated with real estate, which will be discussed later in this chapter, are many. For now, let it suffice to say that most mortgages today exceed the true value of the property that underlies them.

Treasury Bills and Money-Market Funds

Finally, I should mention two Capital Black Hole favorites, Treasury bills and money-market funds. Treasury bills mask the realities of lending money to the government long term, because they are only 90-day instruments. However, if a person were to continually roll his money over in T-bills, "the house" would eventually wipe him out through price inflation. Short-term visits for your money are okay, but don't make the mistake of getting overly relaxed while your capital is in the hands of the government. And never forget that Treasury bills only pay off in *paper.*

Money-market funds are really nothing more than an extra middleman, their sole assets consisting of the paper of other Capital Black Holes. Their advantages are twofold. First, because they deal in large sums of money, they are able to command high rates of interest and thus pay relatively high yields. Second, they offer immediate redemption without penalties. If you wish to park some capital in a fund for a short period of time (and do make sure that it's a short-term proposition), you should make certain to choose a fund with a high-grade portfolio (relatively speaking, that is). In this respect, money-market funds invested solely in Treasury bills are safest; those in CD's and commercial paper (unsecured loans to major corporations) are the most dangerous. In any event, remember that money-market funds, like all Capital Black Holes, pay off only in paper and will therefore ultimately make your capital evaporate.

CAPITAL CRAPSHOOTS

The biggest reasons why the Capital Black Hole alternatives are automatic losers are that they are locked in to a fixed rate of return and they pay off in paper. Thus, corporate stocks deserve the status of Capital Crapshoots, because they are *not* automatic losers like Capital Black Holes; they are only wild speculations. With stocks, you at least have an outside chance—a *very* outside chance—of coming out ahead. Even though any dividends paid will not be sufficient to offset taxes and price inflation, what sets them apart from Capital Black Holes is the possibility for long-term capital gains.

Because there is theoretically an unlimited upside potential, and because capital-gains taxes are much lower than taxes on dividends and interest, it is conceivable that an individual could increase his capital in the stock market. I said there is "theoretically" an upside potential, because all the empirical evidence, as well as the current facts, point overwhelmingly in the opposite direction.

A number of studies, like David Dreman's Contrarian Theory, have shown that a person might very well have equaled, or even bettered, the records of most stock analysts over the years had he simply chosen stocks by donning a blindfold and throwing darts at a stock board. You occasionally hear of a winner here or there, just as you do in a gambling casino, but almost never among the "smart-money experts." I personally have always been of the opinion that an individual has just as good a chance at Caesar's Palace, and he can have a lot more fun in the process.

However, there is an even worse problem than the problems involved in trying to pick the right stocks at the right time: Even if you make a profit, you will be paid off in *paper.* I'm *trying* to be redundant: The objective is to get *out* of paper. The objective is to convert paper into hard assets (i.e., real assets, meaning assets with a utility value).

This point cannot be repeated often enough, because it is a completely foreign way of thinking to most people. Which is exactly why they are going to get caught holding the Old Maid. They keep thinking in terms of paper profits, forgetting that the increased volume of paper they hold is worth less and less each day.

"Tell us, Mr. Tortoise, where did you acquire your expertise
in stock-market analysis?"

The so-called Dow Jones Industrial Average is the stock market's leading delusionary public relations tool. A 1,000 DJIA, or even a 1,500 DJIA, is pure fiction. The truth is that, adjusted for inflation, the DJIA is at about the same level it was in 1913, when the infamous Federal Reserve Act (the legislation that made monetary inflation an easy proposition) was passed. As paper money is inflated out of sight, the stock market will go wild. The DJIA won't have time to catch its breath as it sprints past 2,000, 3,000, 5,000, and higher.

But it's nothing more than playing with numbers. The reason for its unprecedented upsurge will be the very reason that it's an illusion: inflation of paper money. The problem is that when an investor wants to cash out, he will be taking back those same pieces of paper that the stock market rise will be telling him are worthless! Unfortunately, hard-core stock market addicts will not accept this reality until it's far too late. Make sure you're not one of them.

CAPITAL QUESTION MARKS

There are three alternatives for getting out of paper money that, while far from sure things, are not nearly as risky as Capital Crapshoots, *provided you know what you're doing.* For this reason, I refer to them as Capital Question Marks. These include so-called collectibles, commodities, and real estate.

Like stocks, Capital Question Marks, which are not usually tied to a fixed rate of return, afford an owner the opportunity for long-term capital gains. In addition, however, owners of Capital Question Marks hold *real* assets, not paper (or at least have the option to do so). Nonetheless, Capital Question Marks are far from foolproof.

Collectibles

Collectibles encompass such hard assets as diamonds, gemstones, art objects, rare coins, and antiques. All of these derive their values from their limited supply and continuing, though fluctuating, demand. What is good about collectibles, as a group, is that they fluctuate somewhat in line with increases and decreases in the value of paper money. They will therefore almost certainly at least keep pace with price inflation, and, should there be an interim price deflation, the decrease in their dollar prices will probably be no greater than the temporary increase in the value of the dollar. An additional plus for the smaller collectibles, such as diamonds and gemstones, is that they are easy to hide.

What is bad about collectibles is that only a relatively small number of experts really knows much about them, and you cannot become an expert in this area just by reading a few books. It's a full-time job, which means you can rarely feel certain about what you're buying. Further, when you buy and sell in this market, you are usually dealing with that same relatively small number of experts, and thus you tend to end up buying retail and selling wholesale.

Another disadvantage of collectibles is that their markets are fraught with counterfeiting, which means that, unless you're extremely careful, you could end up losing *all* of your capital. Finally, while the smaller collectibles are easier to conceal than other hard assets, they are also less practical in an emergency. It's pretty hard to buy a loaf of bread with a diamond that's worth $25,000. For this reason alone I believe that collectibles are primarily for the well-heeled, and then only if they have access to the expert advice of someone whom they can totally trust.

Commodities

Commodities (and I am using the term loosely here to include not only the normal commodities traded on commodities exchanges, but also strategic metals) also tend to fluctuate, long term, in line with the value of paper money. The main problem with most commodities, however, is the impracticality of actually taking delivery on them. Where are you going to store 10,000 bushels of wheat? Or a carload of pork bellies?

And, if you insist on thinking short term, commodity trading is *really* an area for experts. The odds against even a well-qualified investor making money in short-term commodity trading are staggering—like putting money on one number at the roulette wheel. Occasionally, the payoff may be substantial, but the likelihood is that you'll get wiped out long before it happens.

Real Estate

Real estate is a whole different kind of Capital Question Mark. Now that everyone has once again been reminded that real estate does *not* always go up, and now that gullible, arrogant speculators and thousands of uninformed real estate brokers are back to tending bar and waiting tables, we can settle down to analyzing real estate on a rational basis.

I first began to sense that the real-estate bubble was about to burst when I heard a famous real estate counselor speak at a financial seminar in the summer of 1980. In response to his own rhetorical question about when the real estate bust was going to occur, he replied, with a self-assured air of finality, "Ladies and gentlemen, there's no bust. There is no bust. We have a temporary lull in the market." Those who were naive enough to listen to this kind of nonsense, and base their investment decisions upon it, may now be wondering why I don't just classify real estate as a Capital Black Hole. You certainly couldn't prove otherwise by their results.

But the fact is that real estate is neither a Capital Black Hole nor a Capital Crapshoot. It is a *hard asset,* an asset with an obvious utility value. This, coupled with the fact that, in most cases, it is not restricted to a fixed, long-term rate of return, causes real-estate prices to move *generally* upward in line with price inflation. If that was all there was to it, it wouldn't even be a question mark. Unfortunately, however, it's not that simple.

The real-estate boom of the past forty-some-odd years has been built primarily on a debt pyramid of low-rate, long-term mortgage money. (Whenever I refer to low-rate, long-term mortgate money, you may assume I am talking only about fixed-rate mortgages.) Now that the lending institutions have awakened—very late in the game, as usual (see Capital Black Holes)—this kind of mortgage money has become an extinct animal. The writing was on the wall when the hotshots began touting "creative financing"—i.e., second mortgages, "wraparound mortgages," purchase-money mortgages, and other schemes used by both buyers and sellers to shield themselves from the realities of the marketplace. "Creative financing" is but a euphemism for selling one's property at a decreased price without admitting it to oneself.

As we have continually witnessed during the collapse of Western Civilization, human beings will go to ingenious lengths to prolong the day of judgment. They will do almost anything to keep their illusions alive. Unfortunately, the day of judgment is now coming due for those who foolishly signed short-term balloon notes to purchase real estate; as a result, foreclosures are rising and prices are falling.

I was once so negative on real estate that I was not even willing to consider it as a possible vehicle for escaping paper money. But the early stages of the collapse in real-estate prices have rekindled my interest. It now definitely rates the status of a Capital Question Mark. Fortunes will not only be lost during the coming economic collapse, but made as well. In between the falling bricks and mortar, there will be pockets of opportunity that would not exist during "normal" times. But there are so many uncertainties involved in real estate—much more so than in any other hard-money asset—that one must proceed with extreme caution and patience.

Basically, there are two titanic forces pulling the real estate market in opposite directions. On the one hand, chronic debauching of paper money continues to increase the demand for real estate, just as it does for all hard assets. On the other hand, the engine of the market—inexpensive, long-term mortgage money—has ceased to exist, which decreases demand.

It should be pointed out, however, that this lack of mortgage money also means drastically reduced new construction, which further raises the demand for existing real estate. But not all types of real estate. For example, does the demand for single-family homes really increase when construction decreases? Here, once again, the media have misled the public. They talk incessantly about an aberration called "pent-up demand," which seems to imply that just because someone wants something, that fact alone increases the demand for it.

The media have not yet figured out that sellers do not particularly care whether or not a person *wants* a house, a car, or a television set. What they really want to know is: Does he have the means to *pay for it?* (Desire *plus* means = demand.) And, not surprisingly, deteriorating economic conditions are leaving more and more people with the means to pay for fewer and fewer things—*especially* things as big as houses. Thus, pent-up demand is nothing more than an invention of the media.

Nonetheless, there is the uncertainty of government intervention in the housing market. On second thought, I should refer to it as an *uncertain certainty*. That the government will intervene is not subject to dispute. The only question is when, where, and how? You can be sure that the cries of the voting class will cause white-knight congressmen to come forth with freshly printed paper money to make single-family homes more affordable. They may not blatantly just hand out paper money to the masses, but the effects will be the same. Leave it to politicians to devise a variety of clumsy schemes to accomplish their aim of pacifying voters.

But don't base your real-estate-investment decisions on the hoped-for actions of politicians. The problem is that when Uncle Sam starts passing this paper around, he may not be interested in supporting the particular type of real estate that *you* have invested in. Commercial real estate, for example, may not get subsidized. Any increase in the value of commercial real estate will probably have to come from a combination of two factors: a decrease in construction and an increase in the number of people wanting to trade in their paper dollars for this kind of asset. And keep in mind that, as the economic collapse increases in intensity, there will be less and less tenant demand for office and retail space, which could decrease investor demand (i.e., decrease prices) along with it.

If you are interested in converting paper dollars into commercial property, patience will prove to be a virtue. Opportunities should increase dramatically as things worsen, and ultimately you should be able to buy properties at well below their replacement costs. But regardless of how attractive the bargain, never obligate yourself to a short-term note on the assumption that you will either be able to refinance the property or resell it at a higher price before the note comes due. Both alternatives are highly doubtful, to say the least.

Apartments and low-priced rental homes are much more risky. For nearly fifteen years it has been difficult, if not impossible, to buy *good* apartment buildings that throw off a positive cash flow, because rents have not kept pace with the increased costs of construction, real-estate taxes, and maintenance, not to mention the cost of mortgage money. But now there is an even greater danger—*rent control.*

Because rent control is such an easy target for vote-conscious politicians, you can count on it as a way of life for many years to come. Not just in the People's Republic of Santa Monica (California) and major population centers, but even in small towns all across the country. As word spreads that Brother Bill in Atlanta got the government to hold down his rent, Sister Millie in Wichita will want to be the beneficiary of the same type of thievery in payment for her vote, too.

It is precisely this kind of government meddling that makes real estate such a question mark. While I do believe that there may be routes through the real-estate maze that can lead to preservation of, and even an increase in, capital, these routes are fraught with financial land mines. And, in my opinion, the route laden with the greatest number of explosives is the one marked "apartment buildings for sale." As the economy worsens, there will be some potential money-makers available in real estate, but be *very* careful—especially with regard to rent control.

On the other hand, high-priced homes bought for rental or speculative purposes are an interesting play, because they are unlikely to be subjected to rent control. Nobody cares about protecting "the rich." In addition, remember that "the rich" tend to get richer during a hyperinflation, and it is for this reason that high-priced homes tend to retain much of their value, even while the general housing market is collapsing.

I have noted this phenomenon with great interest while watching the operations of a long-time friend, Dr. Deal, who builds million-dollar-and-up homes in the Ft. Lauderdale–Boca Raton area. While builders are going belly up in record numbers in southern Florida, Dr. Deal's sales continue at a brisk pace. In view of the fact that there is no mortgage money around, it is more than just mildly noteworthy that a majority of his buyers pay all cash.

Observing this situation firsthand has led me to believe that a good vehicle for converting depreciating paper currency into hard assets is, indeed, to be found in high-priced homes *in the right locations.* Since wealthy people do not much care for discomfort, I would restrict such purchases to warm-weather climates.

Obviously, if someone is stupid enough to take back a low-rate, long-term mortgage on a high-priced home that is sound in all other respects, you should hustle him into a closing before he has a chance to read the newspapers and find out what's been happening on planet Earth. The same holds true in those rare instances where you have the opportunity to assume an existing low-rate, long-term mortgage.

Raw Land.   I reject raw land on the grounds (no pun intended) that it is far too speculative during times of crisis. Undeveloped land carries with it an automatic negative cash flow, for one obvious reason—real-estate taxes, with no offsetting income. If the land is financed (keeping in mind my previous caveats about institutional mortgages and creative financing), then your out-of-pocket expenses are even greater.

In addition, the long term on land can be *very* long, sometimes even decades. For the person who can afford to hold on
indefinitely, while paying the taxes and assessments levied against
his land by City Hall, I suppose raw land is a good way to pre-
serve a large amount of wealth for one's children. But there are
not many people who can afford such a luxury.

One final, obvious caveat about real estate: it is illiquid.
Most people know this; it's just that their actions indicate that
they continually forget it. That is why, if you plan to buy your
own home, you should do so only if you intend to stay put for a
while. If you're buying your home for speculative purposes, you
may just as well convert your depreciating paper into Capital
Crapshoots. In the latter case you can at least cut your losses
short and move on when you decide you've had enough. With a
house, as millions of homeowners have discovered to their dismay,
you may not be able to get out when you want to.

CAPITAL GUARANTEES

Contrary to what most people—particularly speculators—would
like to believe, the only way to virtually guarantee the protection
of your capital against the destruction of paper currency is to
convert it to *real* money. That's right, instead of fooling around
with "investments," just use your bogus paper money to buy the
real thing.

What is "real money"? In theory, just about anything of
value can be used as money. In today's Poland, for example, tobacco and alcohol are readily accepted as money; i.e., you can
buy other goods and services with them. They are accepted as a
medium of exchange, whereas everyone knows that the zloty, the
government's mandated paper money, has no intrinsic value.

But tobacco and alcohol, while commanding a certain
amount of respect as mediums of exchange, are far from the best
forms of money. Tobacco can decompose, liquor bottles can
break, and both of them are cumbersome to use when making

purchases. These are just a few of the many reasons why tobacco and alcohol, while superior to paper, are vastly inferior to other kinds of money.

If you are at all tuned in to the so-called hard-money movement, you have heard many times that gold and silver are by far the best forms of money. In my opinion, they constitute the only true Capital Guarantees in existence. (For the sake of brevity, I will for the most part restrict my discussion to gold, but most of what I have to say is also applicable to silver. Gold is a slightly more desirable money than silver, one of the chief reasons being its greater scarcity.)

So much has been written about gold over the past several years that it might seem as though a discussion of it here would be unnecessary. I wish that were true, but, with all due respect to the many brilliant "hard-money" writers who have covered gold extensively, I feel that their readers are still missing the most important point. It's not the technical information imparted by these writers that has been in error; rarely has that been the case. The error lies in their lack of emphasis on the *crux* of the issue. In fact, increasingly over the past couple of years, many of these newsletter writers have been totally *ignoring* the crux of the gold issue.

What particularly disturbs me is that many so-called gold-bugs of yesteryear have now deserted ship. It makes one wonder if they ever really understood the real reasons for buying gold in the first place. It has become chic in hard-money circles to say that gold was a good investment at $35 an ounce, but that the days of the big profits are long since gone. All I can tell you is that if you allow yourself to be influenced by such talk, you will greatly increase your chances of ending up holding the Old Maid. If ever there was an area in which to do the exact opposite of that which government and the media urge you to do, if ever there was an area in which to do the opposite of that which causes failure, that area is the purchasing of gold. But first a little background:

The United States government, in an incredible display of stupidity, has seemingly found endless ways to squander its gold supplies. Back in 1949, the United States Treasury boasted an all-time high of 700 million ounces of the yellow metal. As of the writing of this book, that figure is estimated to be down to 250–350 million ounces.

In the 1950's and 1960's, the government was losing gold to foreign countries by the carload—about 436 million ounces all told. The governments of those foreign countries, for some strange reason, wanted gold instead of paper dollars, so they rushed to redeem their U.S. currency at a furious pace. That all ended on August 15, 1971, when President Nixon declared that the United States would no longer allow foreign governments to redeem their paper receipts (i.e., "dollars") for real money (i.e., gold). In other words, the United States admitted (in doublespeak terms, of course) that it was bankrupt. Its actions announced to the world, once and for all, that its paper money was a lie.

It is interesting to note that the government, in an attempt to demonstrate that it no longer considered gold to be money, finally allowed U.S. citizens to own the metal beginning on December 31, 1974. The ensuing meteoric rise in the price of gold was, of course, a source of great embarrassment to the fiat-money printers in Washington.

Refusing to be upstaged, the government then proceeded to contemptuously dump gold in the open market in an effort to depress the price, and to demonstrate to gold speculators, once and for all, that the paper dollar was king. But, alas, the king had no clothes. The dollar all but turned pink from embarrassment. The more gold the bureaucrats auctioned, the more the price of gold rose.

What these tactics have amounted to is an ongoing attempt on the part of Uncle Sam to demonetize gold. To his dismay, however, these clumsy attacks have instead hastened the day of *gold's demonetization of paper money.* What the marketplace has been telling the government is: "We like you and all that, but, if it's all the same to you, we'd just as soon keep the gold and let you keep the paper. No hard feelings, of course."

The Galbraithian blushes are still to be found all over Washington, yet Washington's contempt for gold grows greater each day. (While temporary downturns in the paper-money price of gold never fail to prompt a chorus of "I-told-you-so's" from paper-money advocates, their joy is always short-lived—and their long-term dismay is a certainty.) Obviously, confiscation of gold is the only weapon left for the government, and you can count on just that at some future date. *Which is all the more reason for you to own gold!* If the government is that intent on taking it away from you, you had better make certain that you have it— and that you keep it away from them. You're going to need it to survive. Above all else in your long-term planning, *don't blow this one.*

Obviously, if gold was as worthless as government and establishment economists would like you to believe it is, South Africa wouldn't be producing 700 tons of it each year. Or the Soviet Union 200 to 500 tons. Even the United States produces about 30 tons annually. Someone—lots of someones—must be awfully interested in owning gold. And those someones go far beyond dentists, jewelry makers, and industrial users. Yet *you* are constantly discouraged, usually by subtle putdowns, from buying gold.

What is it about gold that makes it so special? You've undoubtedly read about its unique characteristics many times. It is portable, easily and precisely divisible by weight, durable, consistent in quality (while not technically inert, it is extremely stable), easily identifiable, and, perhaps most important of all, scarce enough so that it cannot be obtained in great quantities without considerable effort.

As a result of these characteristics, governments throughout the centuries have never found it necessary to force people to use gold as money. People *know* that gold is money. It has evolved as money through the process of supply and demand, notwithstanding paper money's greater convenience as a medium of exchange. The primary reason for gold's evolution into the world's most accepted form of money is that, in addition to being a medium of exchange, it is also a *store of value.*

There is no question that paper money, as a medium of exchange, has made modern society possible. It is by far the most convenient money ever invented. But as a store of value, it is considerably inferior to baseball trading cards. The latter can only be counterfeited illegally; paper money can be counterfeited *legally*—in unlimited quantities.

Though a paper dollar will buy only about 5% of what it could purchase in 1940, an ounce of gold will still buy about the same amount of products and services that it did forty, fifty, or even one hundred years ago. To understand this, you must think of money as an IOU. It's a way of storing wealth that you do not wish to use right now. Gold accomplishes this objective more effectively than any other commodity; paper accomplishes it the least well.

Because of this, you can no longer use paper currency to store what you've earned. The printing presses will destroy it just as surely as if someone had set fire to it, which is precisely why politicians exhort you to "save" it. If they can convince you to keep your savings in the form of paper, they can quietly extract those savings from you through the printing presses (i.e., decrease its value through monetary inflation).

Is it any wonder that politicians hate gold? Gold, in effect, acts as a lie detector. If the United States dollar was *100%* tied to gold (any other kind of gold standard would be merely cosmetic—and meaningless), it would be like asking Tip O'Neill each day, "Tip, you sneaky old buzzard, you—have you tried to steal anyone's hard-earned money today?" If Tip replied, "Golly, no. I'd never do a thing like that," the gold alarm would sound, loud and clear, for everyone to hear. The gold standard would tell the public that sly old Tip had tried to slide one by them once again—that he had voted for a bill that called for handing out newly printed paper money to people who are not producing products or services that other people are *voluntarily* willing to pay for. The gold alarm would have caught him red-handed.

You may conclude that Tip O'Neill is not a big advocate of the gold standard. Nor, with a few notable exceptions, is any other person now in public office. And it is precisely this refusal on the part of the government to acknowledge gold as money that has hastened the destruction of its own fiat currency.

In theory, paper money is fine, provided it is given only to people who produce products and services that other people voluntarily want to buy. So long as a majority of people believe that this is what paper money is used for, they have *faith* in it. Faith is the key to the whole paper-money scheme; it is the key to the stability of *any* kind of money.

People have faith in gold because of the properties we discussed, and because centuries of experience have reinforced that faith. But paper money has none of the desirable qualities of gold, and centuries of experience have belied people's faith in it. Therefore, the value of a paper currency at any given time exists only in the minds of the people who are forced to use it. Once those people lose faith in the currency, the currency ceases to exist—*no matter what laws the government passes.*

By the same token, so long as people have faith in gold, governments cannot eradicate that faith simply by insisting that gold is not money. Vern Myers suggests how silly such governmental attempts are in the following analogy: "A comparable case would be if the U.S. government passed a law which said that parents no longer love their children; the bureaucrats would assure you that children were now only a commodity. After all, isn't it the law? Therefore sell your children."

Certainly all hard-money newsletter writers, and most of their readers, are well acquainted with everything I have discussed up to this point, yet, as I said earlier, they still seem intent on overlooking the *crux* of the gold issue. This is evidenced in many ways. For one thing, their talk always centers on the price of gold, and what that price means in terms of profits or losses. For another, they recommend selling gold because they fear the possibility of a deflation. Also, they say that gold has risen "too high," and that it is therefore too late to buy. Finally, they warn that one of the big drawbacks to buying gold is that it doesn't pay dividends or interest.

"Tip, you sneaky old buzzard, you—have you tried to steal anyone's hard-earned money today?"

In each of these instances, however, they have drawn their readers' attention away from the crux of the gold issue. Gold was never intended to be an "investment." *The crux of the gold issue is that gold is a protective shield—the finest ever known to man— against the destruction of paper currencies.*

Gold is a survival tool. *It guarantees you that the fruits of your labor will not be stolen.* Think of gold as markers; it keeps track of the amount of goods and services you are entitled to as a result of your labor. Governments can print infinite amounts of paper markers, but gold markers cannot be manufactured. You buy gold as a near-foolproof insurance policy against government's paper-money theft scheme; you don't "invest" in gold in the hopes of making profits.

Once a person understands the crux of the gold issue, he has little interest in the paper-money "price" of gold, whether it be $200 an ounce, $2,000 an ounce, or $20,000 an ounce. When the destruction of paper money is nearing its end, gold may very well be "priced" at *$1 million an ounce,* but so what? If the $1 million in paper money buys only a basket of groceries, does the price really matter? You may just as well measure gold in terms of air. If you understand the *long term*—which is the focus of this chapter—you will condition your mind to ignore the "price" of gold in terms of depreciating paper dollars.

Likewise, you will not be tempted to sell gold just because its paper-money price happens to be dropping at any given time. This is where many "deflationists" totally miss the boat. A detailed historical study of gold's effectiveness as a store of value, by Professor Roy Jastram of the University of California (Berkeley), confirms that gold tends to retain its value in relation to other commodities, long term, even through periods of deflation. What does it matter if the paper-money price of gold is $100 an ounce, if one ounce of gold at that price buys the same amount of other commodities as it did at $500 an ounce? Gold transcends paper-money prices; in fact, it really *measures the value of paper money,* rather than the other way around.

As to the argument that it's "too late" to buy gold because

you didn't get in at $35 an ounce, or $100 an ounce, or whatever, you should by this time see the faulty logic in such thinking. Gold is for long-term planning. Just because you didn't get in at the beginning, when the government first removed its artificial price barrier, doesn't mean that it's any less a protective tool now than it was then. Sure it's nice to be able to buy gold at a lower paper-money price, for the obvious reason that you can get more of it with fewer pieces of paper. But how many times in your life have you gotten in on *anything* on the ground floor? Get in *now.* Buy today; buy at $1,000 an ounce; buy at $5,000 an ounce. Let someone else get stuck with the Old Maid.

Finally, there is the argument that gold does not pay dividends or interest. Such an argument could only be made by an individual who does not understand the financial realities of today's world. As I pointed out earlier, virtually none of the traditional investments (so called)—i.e., Capital Black Holes and Capital Crapshoots—is income producing; they all *lose* to price inflation and taxes. It's true that if you're able to pick the right Capital Question Mark at the right time, and watch over it carefully, you have a chance to break even or, conceivably, even make a profit. But what makes gold unique is that the break-even is virtually *assured.*

As to how to buy gold and what types to buy, reams of reading material are readily available to help you in these areas. Not only are there many good books on the market, but any gold dealer will be more than happy to send you detailed literature on the subject.

The South African Krugerrand gets the lion's share of gold's publicity, and, all things considered, it is probably the best vehicle for owning gold. It's a matter of market domination. Just as more people would rather buy IBM or Xerox equipment because they are much better known in the marketplace, and hence more likely to retain higher resale values, so it is with the well-known Krugerrand. South Africa, with its enormous resources of gold (relative to other countries), has effectively dominated the gold-coin market through its Krugerrand. It now also makes 1/10 Krugerrands, 1/4 Krugerrands, and 1/2 Krugerrands, which are convenient for smaller transactions.

(While speaking of lower-value coins, I would like to make a specific point about silver. Because silver's value per unit is much less than that of gold, you will, in the coming years, need a sufficient supply of silver coins for use in day-to-day transactions. The corner grocer may not be able to make change for an ounce of gold. Another advantage is that, even in a deflation, silver coins are never worth less than their face value. Therefore, depending upon your means, you should convert enough paper currency to "junk silver" to meet your small-purchase needs of the future. So-called junk silver consists of pre-1965 silver dimes, quarters, and half-dollars, and is normally sold in $1,000 face-value bags—consisting of 720 ounces of silver.)

In addition to the Krugerrand, other readily recognizable gold coins inlcude the Mexican Peso (10, 20, or 50), the Austrian 100 Corona, the Canadian Maple Leaf, the Hungarian 100 Korona, and the U.S. $20 Double Eagle. Large gold bullion bars (100 ounces) are impractical for most people to hold, one of the chief reasons being that too much value is condensed into a single unit.

Gold is one area where you cannot afford inaction, because, as Gary North has correctly noted, betting against gold is the same as betting *on* governments. And, says North, "He who bets on governments and government money bets against 6,000 years of recorded human history." Those certainly are not the kind of odds you want to apply to your long-term planning.

Gold is the only known method for virtually guaranteeing the protection of your capital from the destruction of paper currencies. I consider this issue to be of such great importance that I have, at the risk of being redundant, summarized below a number of rules you should keep in mind at all times with regard to buying gold.

1. Start buying gold now, *regardless* of the price. By acting now, you will not have to *react* when it's too late. Too late will be when the majority of the public finally figures out what is hap-

pening to paper money and frantically tries to get aboard. Remember, if you're one of the ones holding paper in the end, you will have given away your products and services for nothing.

2. Continue to buy gold on a regular basis, *regardless* of whether the paper-money price goes up or down.

3. When people gab about the price of gold at cocktail parties, neither listen to what they have to say nor offer advice. Entering into discussions with amateur speculators, who jump from one fad investment to another, will only tempt you to take your eye off the crux of the gold issue.

4. Do not buy gold on credit, and never buy options (unless you're doing so just to satisfy your gambling instincts, with the clear understanding that such purchases have nothing to do with the long-term strategy of converting paper currency into real money).

5. Pay for all gold purchases in cash; checks leave a convenient trail for government snoops to follow. When Washington once again decides to confiscate gold, you can be sure that all bank records will be made readily available to bureaucratic henchmen. Likewise, refuse to sign anything when making gold purchases, and certainly do not allow yourself to be fingerprinted (a practice that has already gone into effect in many areas).

6. Do not keep gold or silver in a safe-deposit box. When Confiscation Day arrives, Uncle Sam will surely close all banks and *open* the bank's safe-deposit boxes. If you think this is far-fetched, go back to page one of this book and start from scratch again; you apparently missed something. Banks are completely controlled by the government, and there can be no question that they will fully cooperate with the Feds in a "crisis." Where should you hide your gold and silver? In a place where *I* would never think to look. If you're smart enough to own it, you're smart enough to hide it. I don't want to suggest hiding places to you any more than I want to know your ideas on the subject.

7. Don't talk to anybody about the fact that you own gold or silver, except members of your immediate family (and, even then, be sure that the members who know are emotionally equipped to

be entrusted with such information). When the envy riots begin in earnest, you'll be glad you were prudent about keeping your business to yourself.

If you remember these rules, and act accordingly, you will be way ahead of the vast majority of Western citizens even if you fail to take any of the other actions suggested in this book. By investing in real money, you eliminate virtually all risk and get right to the crux of the issue. In the end, you can absolutely count on gold—*not* paper money—being king.

CHAPTER IX

You Must Be Kidding

Human beings are a strange lot. They will scream bloody murder when subjected to discomfort, yet, within a short time of being relieved of their misery, will show little or no interest in devising ways to avoid such discomfort in the future.

During the gasoline shortages of the seventies, consumers were up in arms and short of temper because of the long service-station lines. After hours of waiting, not only did irritability often lead to fist fights, there were even sporadic reports of people pulling knives and guns. But today, while the nation is experiencing a temporary oil glut, the last thing in the world people are interested in thinking about is a possible future shortage of petroleum products—or future shortages of anything. In fact, I would say that preparing for shortages probably interests fewer readers than any other subject discussed in this section—which from my standpoint is rather frustrating, since I consider it to be *one of the most important subjects in the entire book.*

If your long-term plans do not include a strategy for coping with the severe shortages that are certain to evolve out of the economic turbulence and civil unrest that lie ahead, you need not worry about missing out on any of the social fireworks of the future. You can be sure that you'll be standing in the ration lines, right along with all the rioters, fighting to get your "fair share" of the "necessities" of life.

In reality, of course, there is no such thing as a necessity, for the same reason that there is no such thing as a "need." Within the context of this chapter, *necessities* should be taken to mean the consumer goods that most people have come to rely on; i.e., the specific goods that people most *desire*. These include everything from soap to food, from light bulbs to razor blades, from medicines to clothing—in short, any item that *you* feel you need in order to survive and be comfortable. When a shortage of that item occurs, it simply means that you can no longer buy it at a price you are willing to pay.

Technically, of course, a shortage cannot exist in a free market. That's because as an item becomes more scarce, producers respond by raising the price of that item, and hence fewer people are willing or able to pay for it. Instead, they do without it (heresy in our age of "entitlements"); thus there is no shortage at the higher price. Yet a true free market rarely, if ever, exists for any product, so shortages of various kinds and degrees are not that uncommon. However, as government intervention in the marketplace increases in the coming years, the number and severity of shortages will dramatically increase along with it.

This future scenario of massive shortages is by now an absolute certainty. How am I able to guarantee this? First, because I understand human nature. Second, because I have complete faith in Nature's most basic law: actions have consequences. If you understand human nature, and believe that actions have consequences, there is nothing mystical or complicated about why there will be future shortages of a variety and severity never before thought possible in this country.

The evolution of shortages, reduced to its simplest components, is as follows: The government causes prices to rise by inflating the paper-money supply and handing out the newly created bogus money to nonproducers; people then complain to the government about "mysterious" rising prices; the government in turn steps in and "regulates" prices (i.e., "controls" them); companies and individuals then have no choice but to stop producing the controlled items (or they continue to produce them at the controlled prices, in which case they eventually go broke); as a result, shortages of the controlled items develop (i.e., people cannot find the items for sale at the prices the government has assigned to them); human nature being what it is, people then turn to the government with greater fury than before; the government, instead of admitting that it is responsible for the whole mess and just stepping out of the way, worsens the situation by imposing new laws and regulations, spending more money to cover the costs of enforcing these new laws and regulations, and attempting to ration the controlled items; the ongoing effect, of course, is the creation of ever more numerous and ever worsening shortages.

Does all this mean there is no hope? Fear not—mankind is here. To the age-old annoyance of governments, man is incredibly resilient and resourceful. He progresses *despite* government meddling. His tried-and-true answer to government price controls: "black markets." Much as many of the Big Liars love to sneer at this ominous-sounding term, a black market is really nothing more than a free market reasserting itself in the face of government interference.

What brings a black market into existence are two human realities. First, human beings always strive to find a way to obtain that which they desire; second, someone is always willing to furnish others with a desired product or service at a price that is commensurate with the effort and risk involved. So when government attempts to *control* prices, what it really does is *increase* prices by removing goods and services from the open market and forcing consumers to buy them at higher black-market prices.

Believe it or not, most politicians are very much aware of this reality. But what are their alternatives? Admit that it is they who cause price inflation? Admit that the facade of price controls actually forces prices to go higher? Hardly. Instead, they simply ignore black markets as much as possible, knowing that these markets comprise the only system that can keep a government-strangled economy alive.

Stories abound about flourishing black markets in slave

states like the Soviet Union and Poland. A recent article, for example, described how gas-station attendants in the Soviet Union conspire with gasoline-tank truck drivers to give them unrecorded fuel, which they in turn sell privately. The two conspirators then split the profits. Official figures estimate that 50% to 60% of all gas and oil purchased by Russian automobile owners comes from the black market. The article quoted a Moscow motorist, who laughingly boasted that "whatever diabolical schemes the authorities devise to dry up the supply of (illegal) gasoline, 'the peasants will figure a way around it.' " The government only superficially attempts to disrupt the black market in gasoline, because it is well aware that human nature never changes—i.e., that people will always find ways to get what they want.

If you possess a reasonably good understanding of human nature, and are unyielding in your belief that actions have consequences, you should find it quite difficult to envision a collapsing Western world that is *not* saddled with every conceivable type of shortage. The long-term-planning question for you to answer is, What is the best way to plan for these shortages?

Basically, there are four alternatives. First, you can buy in the black markets as your future needs for various goods arise, which is probably the least time-consuming, but most expensive, solution. Second, you can produce your own products, which is by far the most difficult solution. Third, you can barter with friends and neighbors, which is both a time-consuming and complicated solution. Finally, you can "stockpile" much of what you think you will need in the future, which is practical, relatively simple, involves comparatively little time, and is by far the least expensive solution.

BLACK MARKETS

We have already discussed how black markets come into existence. You can be sure that as conditions deteriorate, you will have easy access to all types of black markets. While publicly espousing its evils, even liberals, the media, and bureaucrats will participate in black-market "shopping" in their normal course of living. The problem, as I said, is that the black market is very expensive. It's nice to know that black markets will exist so long as man exists, but, if you plan wisely for the long term, you can avoid having to make all of your purchases through this costly medium in the years ahead.

It goes without saying that, as the final destruction of Western currencies nears, gold and silver will become the primary means of payment in the black markets. Black-market operators are far too smart to accept paper money during a hyperinflationary debacle. They will fully appreciate the fact that their very existence is due to the worthlessness of paper money.

PRODUCING YOUR OWN PRODUCTS

Producing your own products is scary to most people in our modern age of specialization, and rightly so. It is because of the division-of-labor concept that we have reached our present living standard. For each of us to produce most of the things we use daily would be totally impractical.

Nevertheless, one would be prudent to acquire at least some rudimentary production skills. Just because you don't know how to operate a farm doesn't mean you can't learn to grow some vegetables. Just because you don't know how to build a house doesn't mean you can't learn to construct a table. Just because you don't know how to make a pair of slacks doesn't mean you can't learn to repair a damaged garment. Where you draw the line on this matter (and I suspect many people will draw it at zero) is, as always, something you must decide for yourself. But it doesn't take much time, effort, or money to buy some basic tools, study a few books, and practice a little in your spare time. Every self-sufficiency skill you gain will make it that much easier for you and your family to survive the widespread shortages of the future.

BARTERING

Bartering is as old as civilized man. Before money came into existence, the only way men could trade with one another was through barter. As the destruction of paper currencies accelerates, and shortages become more widespread, barter will become more and more common. (Remember, most people will not have had the good sense to convert their paper dollars into gold and silver, thus they will have no means of purchasing in the black markets.)

It will be relatively easy to know the barter price of a product or service, because the barter marketplace—which will, in essence, be unregulated—will automatically set all prices through the wondrous workings of supply and demand. As the number of people who participate in bartering increases, the pricing mechanism will become ever more precise. You will learn relatively quickly how many cans of Ovaltine are needed to buy a bottle of Chivas Regal. To one extent or another, you *will* be bartering in the future, whether or not you plan to, so it would be a worthwhile investment of your time to read up on the subject.

STOCKPILING

Paradoxically, stockpiling is not only the best solution to the problem of shortages, but the least accepted one. In other words, most people consider it to be the least appealing solution to a problem that (unfortunately) is of little interest to them to begin with. I know this to be true because of the reactions I've observed in discussing this topic with others.

Why should the *best* solution be the *least* accepted? Because stockpiling requires *specific* and *immediate* action. Buying in the black markets is something you don't have to worry about until the time comes that you have to make your first purchase. Nor do you have to give any serious thought right now to producing your own products; you can just make a token gesture toward that end by buying a few tools and books. And to prepare for bartering, you need only buy some literature on the subject and put it on the bookshelf. But stockpiling is a way of saying, "I'm really serious about surviving future shortages, and I'm going to get started *now.*"

Stockpiling is simply the act of buying goods, preferably in large quantities, far in advance of the time you think you will need them. I've been doing it for years, on a small scale, without even being conscious of it. For example, it seems that whenever I find an item I particularly like, the manufacturer has an annoying habit of either discontinuing it or changing (lowering) its quality. To offset this problem, I often stock up on such an item, thereby assuring myself that I will have it, when I want it, for many years to come.

It wasn't until I read John Pugsley's comprehensive work, *The Alpha Strategy,* that I realized I had only scratched the surface of stockpiling. This remarkable book, probably the best ever written on the subject of stockpiling, made me see the logic in expanding upon the stockpiling principle I had already sporadically been using.

What's nice about stockpiling is that not only do you guard against shortages, you are also circumventing the paper-money problem in the simplest way possible. When you buy goods in advance, you skip the in-between step of converting to real money (i.e., gold or silver). Instead, you go straight to the products you would eventually buy with your gold or silver anyway. In addition, stockpiling not only protects you against future price increases, but, because you are purchasing in relatively large quantities, you're usually able to demand lower prices. Most important, though, you are ensuring that you will have the item when you need it.

Naturally, there are also disadvantages to stockpiling. The primary ones are inadequate or unsuitable storage space, decomposition (to varying degrees and over various periods of time, depending on the product), and the threat of theft. It has been my experience that even the small number of people who are, at the

"Hi, T.T., old buddy. I just been tellin' the local commissar here about all them goodies you been storin' away for years."

outset, somewhat open-minded toward stockpiling usually lose interest once these negatives are pointed out. And that, indeed, is illogical.

Just because there are problems (as there are with any solution) is no reason to lose out on the *benefits* of stockpiling. Just because space limitations, decomposition, and the threat of theft—not to mention limited resources—prevent you from stockpiling the optimum varieties and quantities of items you would like to stockpile is not a sound reason for not stockpiling *some* things in *some* quantities. It's better to have a six-month supply of dehydrated food than none at all. It's better to have a good supply of spark plugs than no auto supplies at all. It's better to have a modest supply of batteries with a one-year shelf-life than no batteries at all. Stockpiling, in other words, does not have to be an all-or-nothing proposition. Any steps you take, no matter how small, will be steps in the right direction.

As with converting paper money to gold and silver, the important thing with stockpiling is to *get started*. Begin on a small scale and sustain your purchasing program at a pace that is comfortable for you. Do it *regardless* of how crazy your friends may think you are. If your friends look at you incredulously and say, "You must be kidding," that may only mean that you need new friends—friends who are more knowledgeable about how the world works. Just remember, the friend or acquaintance who snickers at your long-term-planning measures is the same person who will be banging on your door at some future date, with the local commissar at his side, demanding access to all the goodies you've stockpiled inside your abode.

If you can't seem to muster an interest in preparing for future shortages, I suggest you study up on economics and human nature (a little history would also be helpful); it will do wonders for stirring your motivation. You must figure severe shortages into your long-term planning. Now is the time to do something about this guaranteed future problem, while most people are half asleep and totally ignoring it. Now is your chance to make substantial headway, with the least amount of effort, at the lowest cost. Once the shortages begin, it will be much more difficult to accomplish your aims.

While I strongly recommend stockpiling, I realize that the chances are good that you will not act on my advice. In that event, the least you should do is study up a bit on bartering and begin to learn some rudimentary self-sufficiency skills like growing food and making clothes. And, if you're not willing to do even that, just start *thinking* about shortages. When you picture a potential problem in your mind, it has a way of making you better prepared to handle it when the time comes. And it *is* coming!

CHAPTER X

Pleasant Dreams, Grosse Pointe

I presume that if you were concerned enough to buy this book, you are already well aware of the violence that now exists in America and other Western nations. If there were no increase in such violence in the future, what we already have would be sufficient reason to write this chapter.

But the violence *will* increase—to an extent that is hard for most people to fathom. The violence that presently surrounds us has a more or less random quality, but, as the economy that feeds our desires-are-rights society continues to come unglued, the violence will become more purposeful. In the future, it will be motivated first by deepening envy, and, finally, by outright survival.

The average Western man is not prepared for this. He is not even prepared for the violence that already surrounds him. Most people, for example, would not dream of spending a few thousand dollars on a good home-security system to protect the lives of their families. Yet these same people scarcely blink at spending a similar amount on a vacation. Vacations, after all, are a necessity.

Your willingness to prepare for the widespread civil disorder and rioting of the future really depends upon whether or not you believe that there will be a complete destruction of Western paper currencies and whether or not you understand that severe shortages are an inevitable consequence of such a destruction. If you don't, then the rest of this chapter will not be very meaningful to you. But if you understand and believe that such a scenario is inevitable, logic obliges you to conclude that social chaos and violence must follow. And a rational man does not ignore such a threat; he prepares for it—far in advance, if possible.

Aside from discretion and good old common sense, the importance of which I cannot overemphasize, there are two basic components of a sound self-defense program: geography and weapons.

GEOGRAPHY

Most people have never given any thought to moving to another city, let alone another country. Either they unthinkingly accept their circumstances or they use the old standby excuse that "the timing isn't quite right." Such people would do well to face the reality that "the timing" is not going to improve in the future; on the contrary, it will only get worse.

The self-imposed immobility of human beings is a curious phenomenon. The German Jews of the late 1930's were a prime example. On hindsight, it is easy for people to find it inconceivable that, after Hitler came to power and made his grisly intentions so clear, Jews did not emigrate from Germany en masse. But, like everyone else, those Jews had businesses and relatives and friends; "the timing wasn't quite right." And, besides, Germany was "home."

We may never be subjected to the same systematic genocide in this country (though we should not be so apathetic or naive as to assume that it could not happen here), but if one respects the empirical evidence as indicative of what the accelerating collapse of Western Civilization holds in store for us, prudence would dictate that he move to the safest, most comfortable geographic area possible.

There are any number of personal reasons why an individual may prefer one area of the country (or world) to another. These may include such things as family ties, "culture," religion, availability of entertainment, characteristics of the people in a given locale, conveniences of various kinds, and general lifestyle. Only you are in a position to give proper weight to your preferences and biases in these and other areas. In contemplating relocation of yourself and your family, however, there are certain considerations that I feel are of special importance, in view of worsening conditions in the Western world. It is to these considerations that I will address myself in the following pages.

Climate

A majority of people in this country are "trapped" in cities where the weather is unbearably cold and wet in winter and blisteringly hot and humid in summer. The fact that many of the most dangerous cities in America are situated in these foul-weather areas, yet millions of people choose to remain in such cities, is rather overwhelming evidence that a large percentage of human beings find ways to accept their fate in life, no matter how grim.

While climate involves day-to-day comfort, and thus must be viewed as an integral part of your life, it should not rate as more than a tie breaker, as it were, when it comes to making a final relocation decision. After all, there are hundreds of millions of people all over the world who live in warm-weather climates, but are enslaved. You should weigh all other important factors before focusing on weather.

Cost of Living

Generally speaking, the bigger the city, the higher the cost of living. The reasons for this are obvious, beginning with supply and demand. Job opportunities and the "excitement" of a big city attract a steady stream of people to major metropolitan centers, which translates into more people bidding up the prices of products and services. Further, the increased crime and other social problems that plague these areas raise government operating costs, and thus indirectly add to the cost-of-living burden by bringing about higher taxes.

The cost of living in some major cities is now so astronomical that it has become a major consideration in deciding whether or not to relocate. In Los Angeles and San Francisco, for example, the costs of the barest necessities of life are in no way related to the real world. As my good friend, Baby Huey, pointed out some time ago, most people now residing in major population centers in California are living in self-imposed poverty. I had never thought of it in that light before, but he's absolutely right. People who live in such cities are either very rich, very poor, or very masochistic.

Interestingly, climate and cost of living are very much related, as is evidenced by the devastating economic realities of life in Southern California. The mild climate of that area heightens the demand to live there, which not only drives up the prices of real estate and all other products and services, but puts local governments in a position to practice extortion. Politicians unashamedly exploit the demand for living in Southern California by increasing taxes and other forms of theft to the maximum the market will bear.

Those who choose to remain in such an area have, indeed, made the decision to live in self-imposed poverty, though this decision may not have been a conscious one. It has not yet dawned on them that by moving to another city, they might considerably upgrade their standard of living. A decrease in the cost of living is the equivalent of an increase in pay, so long as any decrease in income that may result from moving to another city is not substantial enough to offset it. Where businesses are concerned, many have found that their revenues are as high, or higher, after moving their operations to a smaller city, while they enjoy a dramatic decrease in operating expenses.

Civilian and Government Crime

I group civilian and government crime together, because it makes no real difference whether it's your neighbor or a bureaucrat who commits aggression against you.

Once again, California is a test-tube example. While "the poor" in jungles like New York and Chicago are militant, in California they go one step further—they are *arrogant*. In Southern California, in particular, welfare recipients visit Disneyland and Magic Mountain, sunbathe and surf at the beaches, and attend big-league sporting events. Wild hairdos, one earring, gold neck-chains, and scraggly jean outfits are in; humility is out. But what else would you expect from a city like Los Angeles—the only place in the world where Hare Krishnas are considered establishment.

To keep these people—the core of the voting class—happy, someone must pay. And nice fellows like Leonid Cranston are always around to make sure that the proper arrangements are made. Since the state and city governments can't print money, they collect it: through income taxes, estate taxes, inventory taxes, sales taxes, personal-property taxes—there's no end in sight. The California state income tax alone is a whopping 10%. And you can forget about old-fashioned procedures like tax-loss carry forwards—or backwards. Just shut up and hand over the money; they don't want to hear about the million dollars you lost last year.

One thing you must admit about the California socialists who hold the reins of power is that they don't fool around. They make no attempt whatsoever at subtlety. California has organizations you would assume are funded by the Kremlin. Try the State Board of Equalization on for size. Or the California Coastal Commission, which is even worse. The latter specializes in extortion, like refusing to allow a builder to build an oceanfront hotel unless he sets aside a certain number of rooms for "the poor." Or sometimes the bureaucrats will just settle for an outright payoff, usually in the form of a land "contribution"—and always, of course, for "the poor."

The state of New York is even worse on the income-tax theft, taking up to 14% from producers. Now that takes incredible arrogance on the part of its politicians, considering the fact that a majority of its citizens live in the greater New York City area. It would be one thing to be forced at gunpoint to live in New York, but to have the audacity to up the ante for the privilege of living in a sewer is bold indeed.

Yet, when you stop to think about it, what other choice do New York's rulers have? The masses have been literally tearing New York City apart for years, and someone has to pay for the repairs, as well as furnish living expenses for the nonproducers. So long as tens of thousands of producers insist on living in New York, they must face the reality that they constitute the city's primary source of income.

As economic conditions in all Western nations continue to deteriorate, you can count on rioting on a scale previously unimagined. The big-city riots of the 1960's were but foreshocks of the major social quakes that lie ahead. The Miami riots of 1980 and 1982 were preliminary warning signs that things are beginning to heat up.

A few years ago, when the Red Baron maintained a home in Beverly Hills, his housekeeper told him that the Los Angeles rioters of 1965 realized that they had made a mistake by inflicting their damage on Watts. "The next time," she confided to him, "they'll come marching into places like Beverly Hills." The Red Baron, who didn't make his fortune by ignoring pragmatism, packed up, sold out, and jetted off to one of his other homes around the world.

Remember, even though the politicians created the chaos, they are also stuck with the problem of how to deal with it. That means not only higher and higher taxes, but more and more restrictions, laws, regulations, and general government harassment. I say "general harassment," because I don't think the average person can imagine the goodies his government will have in store for him—particularly in major cities—when things really begin coming apart.

Gary North has suggested what one such tactic might be, and, on hindsight, it is quite obvious. If the local government doesn't think you're cooperating as you should, all it need do is have your gas, electricity, water, and/or telephone shut off. Are you prepared to handle *that* for a few days? Or weeks? Or months? If your answer is no, you'd better stop snickering and, instead, start analyzing the feasibility of moving to a safer city, assuming you're presently living in a major metropolitan area. And, wherever you move, start thinking about the installation of emergency water and power facilities.

Of course, municipal workers will probably beat the government to it. When it gets to the point that they're getting paid in money that no one else will accept, doesn't it make sense that they'll just stop working? Try to picture New York, Boston, or Pittsburgh without gas, electricity, water, or sewage for a long period of time. Try real hard, because you can bet that you're going to see it in your lifetime. And I'm not talking about the minor city-worker strikes you've witnessed in the past. I'm talking about full-scale anarchy.

Another possible "emergency" tactic is that the government may find it "necessary" to move "needy" people into your house. Why in the world should a family of four be living in a mansion in Scarsdale when thousands are without a roof over their heads? As Dr. Zhivago conceded, the arrangement would be much more equitable if living space were equally divided. Keep chuckling, but, in between chuckles, do yourself a favor and engage in some serious thinking about how prepared you are to cope with such an eventuality.

If you are hopelessly attracted to the big city, you should also keep terrorism in mind. (Terrorism is simply violent crime on a better organized, more sophisticated level.) Anyone who snickers at terrorism is not just naive; he's been living on another planet. Terrorism is a fact of twentieth-century life.

Now use some common sense. Where do you think terrorists are going to strike when things heat up? Des Moines? El Paso? Fargo? Where would *you* strike if you were a terrorist bent on doing the greatest possible damage while grabbing the biggest possible headlines? Pleasant dreams, Grosse Pointe.

This is not to imply that small cities will be completely immune to trouble. The anything-goes mentality will convert empty stomachs into envious minds everywhere. It's just that the problems inherent in such a scenario will be substantially compounded in larger cities.

If you're a hoodlum in Chicago who's looking for food, or a television set, or just plain trouble, are you going to take the time to drive to a small town in lower Wisconsin to satisfy your needs? It may happen occasionally, but the odds are against it. Why undertake a lengthy journey when those "greedy capitalists" in Evanston are just up the road? After all, they're the ones who have caused all your problems, anyway. (Their real sin, of course, is that they're highly visible. Obviously, it's wise to keep a low profile in our anything-goes age.)

Nuclear War

A more remote reason for considering relocation is the threat of nuclear war. It is interesting to note how millions of people throughout the Western world take the threat of nuclear war seriously enough to participate in demonstrations, sign petitions, and make their feelings known in surveys, yet few of them are serious enough to take personal precautions.

If you talk to an anti-nuclear-weapons demonstrator about moving to a safer location, he will likely look at you as though you're some kind of crackpot. In reality, though, it is he who's the crackpot: At the same time that he insists an attack could begin at any moment, he lacks the good sense to get out of the line of fire. It makes one wonder if such people really believe what they're preaching.

Perhaps the best book ever written on the subject of protecting yourself and your family in the event of a nuclear attack is Dr. Bruce Clayton's *Life After Doomsday*. It's a rational, fact-filled text that covers, in an easy-to-read manner, just about everything you need to know about how to survive a nuclear attack. Clayton pinpoints southwestern Oregon and northwestern California as the only areas of the United States that are unlikely to receive

*"You must admit, Dr. T., that this is a much more equitable
arrangement—is it not?"*

any nuclear fallout in the event of nuclear war. In addition, Western Canada and Mexico, south of Monterrey, are seemingly safe. A good portion of Wisconsin, particularly the central and eastern regions, as well as small pockets in Iowa and Wyoming, are secondary possibilities.

I know from past experience that few people are seriously interested in pursuing this subject, so I will not engage in further discussion here. However, if you wish to acquaint yourself with the ways and means to protect yourself and your family from nuclear horrors, I highly recommend Dr. Clayton's book.

Occupation

As with climate, occupational considerations should be subordinated to considerations of safety. Of what value is a good-paying job or a profitable business if you don't survive to enjoy it? Or, worse, if you do survive, but do so in a living hell? In the coming years, millions of people will be trapped in urban nightmares because they allowed their jobs to be the major determinant of where they should live.

First and foremost, and this rule would apply even if Western Civilization were not collapsing, don't become emotionally attached to your occupation, whether it's a job or your own business. This may not be something you want to hear, but it's something you would be well-advised to think about. The primary reason that it is unwise to become emotionally attached to your occupation is that government, which is always changing the rules of the game, will be changing them fast and furiously as things get out of hand. As a consequence, it can destroy your business or profession literally overnight.

If you're a doctor, for example, you ought to begin thinking of socialized medicine as a future certainty. If you intend to stay married to your profession, you had better love your work more than your pay. If you're a real estate broker or a builder, you've already had a couple of previews of what government meddling in the economy can do to your income. The same is true of virtually any trade or profession; no business or industry is immune to government aggression. And, of course, the collapse of any segment of the economy creates a ripple effect that destroys other industries and jobs all down the line.

You may like your work, but it would be judicious to keep one eye on other opportunities, particularly if you go along with the logic of moving to a smaller city. It is, of course, quite possible that whatever it is you presently do for a living may not be practical in a small town. But it is also possible that there may be much greater opportunity in another field of endeavor in a smaller city. Be flexible.

One avenue you should seriously consider is to work extra hours at building another business as a hedge, while continuing to earn a living in your present occupation. I'm not talking here about dabbling. I'm talking about working at only *one* other thing, and working *hard.* Most important, unlike the dabblers of the world, don't look to your second job, business, or occupation as a source of current income. Plant the seeds and give the new venture room to breathe—and grow. Draining away money from a fledgling enterprise is like cutting off its oxygen. If you milk it for current income, it will most likely fail. Forget about getting rich overnight. Lay a solid foundation, then build a solid structure on top of it—over a reasonable period of time.

At the very least, your second occupation should represent an insurance policy. At best, it should represent a way out of your present job or business if it grows to the point that it can support you in a style that satisfies your needs.

The kinds of businesses you might consider during these perilous times are as varied as your imagination. Remember, people are going to need lots of help as Western Civilization continues to unravel, so help them—at a profit. I don't know what your talents are, but you do. Just apply them in a field where you believe government interference will be at a minimum.

I used to believe that the wisest approach was to go into a business that catered to society's lowest common denominator—à la inexpensive motels, fast-food chains, gambling casinos, amusement parks, and the like. But the halcyon days are on the way out. Step by begrudging step, the masses are learning to accept the fact that the party is over. It's not that they've suddenly become prudent; they simply have no other choice. Eviction notices and pink slips have a way of sobering up even the most entertainment-hungry nonproducers. I would be very leery of any business that is dependent upon attracting and keeping a broad base of consumers—particularly destitute consumers.

Of course, if the product or service is something that the welfare planners think the average person "needs," they will try to see to it, through the use of force, that he gets it. But at whose expense? Fuel is a good example. When I warned Black Bart of some of the upcoming dangers in our economy, he profoundly replied: "No matter what happens to the economy, I reckon people will always need to keep warm. That's why I'm in the gas business."

On the surface, I agree. But we've already seen what the Washington dragon can and will do if the voting class begins to exert political pressure for cheap fuel. The windfall-profits tax was just a preview of coming events. As gas and oil companies raise their prices in an effort to share the burden of this onerous tax with consumers, the government, under pressure from the masses, will put these companies in a vise by clamping down on prices. And that will be a good time to be *out* of the gas and oil business. Count on it happening, and relatively soon. Knowing Black Bart's legendary sense of timing, I'm sure he will be long gone from the gas business when it does.

I like occupations and businesses that meet two criteria. First, and ideally, they should be capable of being operated from virtually anywhere. Second, they should cater to a select market, preferably people who have the means to pay for the product or service you're offering. Being an author is one obvious occupation that fits these criteria. Certain types of publishing are another. So are many kinds of mail-order businesses and service companies. This is where your individual talents, preferences, and imagination come into play. Once you open your mind to new possibilities,

I think you'll find it exciting to review all the options that are available to you. But you *must* open your mind.

One last thing you might want to carefully consider when thinking about a new occupation is the division-of-labor problem. Either you should choose a field that requires very little labor other than your own, or select a geographic area where you have reason to believe that there is an abundance of qualified people who, for whatever strange reasons, still insist on wanting to work for a living. (I understand that many Mormons still suffer from this anachronism, which makes Utah well worth considering.)

As the Western world continues to lurch under the force of greater and greater social tremors, you would do well to acquaint yourself with the political persuasions of those whom you hire. Remember, today's white-collar workers are graduates of American universities heavily staffed with socialist thinkers. They know all the laws regarding hiring and firing. They know all the laws regarding their "rights." They will not hesitate to turn on you when things get out of hand, so don't kid yourself on this point. The failure to consider this danger will be the undoing of many naive businessmen in the years ahead. And it goes without saying that under no circumstances should you become involved with the ultimate menace to economic progress—labor unions.

Now, taking into consideration all of the factors we've discussed, where *is* the best place to live? About all I can reasonably hope to accomplish in this chapter, with regard to that question, is to do a cursory review of some of the more important areas that should be seriously considered, as well as those that should be eliminated. Some places, of course, are so obvious that they don't even need to be discussed. You certainly don't need me to tell you to avoid areas like Afghanistan, El Salvador, or Cleveland—*especially* Cleveland.

Foreign Countries

Foreign countries constitute an alternative that few people are even willing to think about. Understandably, it's a traumatic alternative. Still, it's one you should at least keep on the back burner—just in case. A little study of countries that might interest you—and visiting such countries, if possible—is a good idea, so you won't be starting from scratch if you ever reach the conclusion that things are getting a little too out of hand in the United States. You often hear people say that if the United States goes under, the whole world will go with it. Maybe, but maybe not. Why close off any possibilities?

I personally like what is happening in some parts of Southeast Asia. Singapore, Taiwan, and Hong Kong are capitalist paradises (although it is true that Hong Kong has just recently begun to experience the beginnings of the voting-class problem). Hong Kong has the Red China reunion party coming up in 1997, but that situation is beginning to look less and less ominous as time goes on. Communist China, to the irritation of its hard-line neighbor, the Soviet Union, is now beginning to see the free-enterprise light. The Chinese have proved to be both industrious and intelligent throughout the centuries, which is why I believe they were able so quickly to see the fallacies in communism. By contrast, the Russians as a whole have never been known for their ambition or their gray matter. They aren't exactly what you would call an exciting people. History indicates that the Russian prefers to be ruled and regulated.

Just below Southeast Asia, geographically, is perhaps the Brigadoon of the future—Australia. When I visited Australia a few years ago, I admittedly was disappointed by the socialistic tilt of the people. But all that could change in the future. Socialist countries, in order to survive, need the help of capitalist countries (for the obvious reason that socialism does not work as an economic system). And as Australians—14 million of them in an area approximately the size of the United States—enjoy the advantage of watching Western capitalist countries topple from a safe distance of 8,000 miles or so, they may have a tendency to become increasingly nationalistic. Because of their remote geographical location, they can afford such a luxury. Why get involved with the rest of the world if the rest of the world is going

"I beg of you, sir. Send me anywhere—Afghanistan, El Salvador, Lebanon—anywhere but Cleveland."

up in smoke? But to actually survive on its own, Australia will be forced to drop its socialistic practices and turn to a more capitalistic way of doing business.

Keep an eye on Australia. It may end up being a good long-term play. Remember, this is an isolated country in the South Pacific *that speaks English.* That is no small consideration, because trying to learn a new language is one of the greatest traumas of moving to a foreign country.

Though Costa Rica was, until recently, considered a capitalist haven, I would stay away from Central America unless I were a high-paid mercenary. This area is starting to look more and more like the Middle East, with communist guerrillas and right-wing militias blowing up each other, as well as civilians, at a furious pace.

South America, on the other hand, should remain under consideration, because the countries there, with the exception of a brief interlude in Chile, seem to have a knack for putting down voting-class revolutions and muddling through. The climates are generally warm and the costs of living generally low. Unlike Australia, however, the economies are chaotic, English is not the native tongue, and they are relatively close to the collapsing Western world (not to mention Central America). The countries of South America are a much longer shot than Australia, but I would advise not eliminating them just yet.

I would rule out all of Europe, for three reasons. First, it's too close to the paranoid Russian Bear, who has been known to dispatch troops to neighboring countries at the drop of a freedom sticker. Second, Europe's close proximity to the Soviet Union (part of which is actually in Europe) makes it a likely target for a "limited" nuclear war. Third, Europe's governments are even farther down the dead-end socialist road than the United States, so why bother? You can stay right here in your homeland and enjoy the same traumas.

South Africa is an exciting possibility. I've never been there, but everyone I know who has made the trip says that it's the last frontier of freedom. In the face of the most defamatory press imaginable, it is absolutely remarkable what the people of South Africa have accomplished. The major question, however, is whether or not this nation can stand alone against the rest of the world. Everything possible is being done to stack the deck against South Africa, so it will be interesting to see what happens.

There are, of course, a number of little-known, out-of-the-way places a person might flee to, but most of them are impractical for a Westernized man. However, if such possibilities interest you, you may, in particular, want to study up on small, South Pacific islands. But be prepared for unexpected traumas, because the rules are completely different. Governments there may not be as overt when it comes to taking your money, but they may have a bias toward your head instead.

In the Atlantic Ocean, you might want to consider the Bahamas and the Cayman islands, plus a variety of small Caribbean islands. These are, for the most part, hot, humid places that can become rather dull after about three hours. Cuba is a lovely spot, providing, of course, that you're into repression and can speak Spanish.

As to the United States's neighbors, there are very few advantages. The left-wing revolution is already beginning to rumble in Mexico, so its previous advantages are either gone or on the way out. Canada offers less crowded metropolitan centers and more wide open spaces, but it's just a minor-league version of the U.S. There are enough sparsely populated areas here to choose from, so why go to a country that's just a good imitation of the real thing?

That pretty much covers the foreign possibilities, unless you're interested in places like India, Tanzania, or Antarctica. When one realizes how restricted his relocation options are, it certainly drives home the reality that the world really is a very small place indeed.

I have been as brief as possible on this subject, knowing that few readers will even consider moving to a foreign country. However, if you're one of the few who does have a serious interest in pursuing it, there is one book, above all, that you must read. That is Douglas Casey's *The International Man.* This text will tell you everything you need to know—taxes, governmental structures. social environment, and much more—about any country that may interest you.

United States

In considering relocation to another area of the United States, the nice thing is that there is much less uncertainty involved. Not only do you know much more about this country than any other, but it's considerably easier to gain additional knowledge about any area you may be interested in. For that matter, it's relatively simple, and inexpensive, to personally visit just about any city in the country. And while the governments here, like all governments, are dishonest and capricious, you're at least familiar with how they operate. Even though a foreign government may hold itself forth as "democratic," it's always dangerous to assume that its crimes and follies are no different than those of Uncle Sam and his state and local contemporaries.

Since you must give proper weight to such considerations as family ties, religion, entertainment, conveniences, climate, occupation, and the like, all I can do, once again, is make broad recommendations. The two considerations that are most important to me are civilian crime (including terrorism) and government harassment. The threat of nuclear war is also important, but unless it's your primary concern, you may have to compromise somewhat on this point.

I don't recommend heading for the hills, as it were, because being alone in a remote area could be dangerous if an occasional gang *does* decide to drive up from Chicago. I much prefer small towns, as I'm sure you've gathered by now. The smaller the city, and the further it is from a major metropolitan area, the better. For all the reasons I've discussed, crime and civil disorder will only become worse in the larger cities as time goes on. And, for virtually the same reasons, both local and federal governments will get tougher and bolder when it comes to aggressing on indi-

"Gee, E. C., I like their digital watches, but there's something about the South Pacific that's unsettling."

vidual rights. While martial law will probably go into effect nationwide when the real social fireworks begin, martial law in Duluth will be quite different from martial law in Philadelphia.

Why? Because governments have limited resources, and they will have their hands more than full cracking the whip in battlegrounds like Miami, Baltimore, and Boston. That will make it more difficult to monitor people in small towns, and a natural result may be that small-town folks will develop a collective attitude of "us against the feds." At the very least, it's highly unlikely that you'll see widespread rioting and looting in many smaller cities, while such a scenario is a virtual certainty in major urban centers.

If you just can't bring yourself to move to a small city, then the least you should try to do is move to a city that may be less dangerous than the one you are now living in. For starters, let's eliminate the worst locations.

It should be quite obvious by now that my choices for the three most dangerous cities in the United States are Los Angeles, New York, and Chicago, in that order. I realize that giving Los Angeles a slight edge over New York for the Grand Collapse Award may offend some New Yorkers, but I firmly believe that my reasoning is sound.

I have always viewed New York as the forerunner of the collapse of Western Civilization, a preview of what the Western world is in for when the social structure has totally disintegrated. But that's just the point. New York has been the social cesspool of the nation for so many years that the people who reside there have, in a perverse sort of way, become accustomed to it. The middle and lower classes have been downtrodden for so long that they've almost come to accept misery as a way of life—a sort of collective psychocybernetics. They are used to their misery!

But in Los Angeles, as I pointed out earlier, those at the lowest end of the income spectrum have actually been pampered. It's still fun and sun in Smog City. You don't need to spend your welfare checks on heavy clothing and heating fuel, because the climate is mild. Instead, you can invest in video recorders (replete with porno cassettes), motorcycles, and surfboards. Now, however, the natives are starting to get restless as they see their television sets and motorcycles being repossessed. They are not psychologically prepared to start living like their counterparts in New York. And unless *you* are ready to explain to them that the party is over, unless *you* are ready to relate the economic facts of life to them, you would be wise to keep your distance.

Chicago is New York all over again, but on a slightly smaller scale, thus its relegation to a lowly third position. What can I say about Chicago? It has all the disadvantages of New York, and none of the advantages of Los Angeles. If you now live there, move! You can enjoy the fireworks much better by reading about them in the *Pueblo Star Journal.*

Philadelphia, Baltimore, Boston, Washington, Pittsburgh, and other large cities all have the same problems as the Big Three, only on a smaller scale. It's hard to say which ones will be worst hit, because there are an infinite number of factors to consider that are unique to each city.

The unique factor in Detroit, of course, is obvious, and the coming funerals of Ford and Chrysler (General Motors?) may bring about conditions that will ultimately allow Detroit to edge out Chicago for the number-three slot. Likewise, Miami's unique problems have been well publicized, and, if you're living there, you don't need me to expound on those problems. You need me to remind you to get your affairs in order and get out!

Are there any large cities that will be safe? Answer: No! But a few have a chance of muddling through with much less devastation than those I've named. As a general rule, large cities in the West and Southwest will fare much better than those in the industrial Midwest and Northeast. It's a matter of the desires-are-rights evolution. The "civilizations" of the Midwest and Northeast are much older than those of the Southwest and West, thus they have had more time to evolve from individual sovereignty to lynch-mob rule.

The voting classes in places like Dallas, Houston, and Denver are just now beginning to demand their "rights." Until recently, there was so much opportunity in those cities that people had little motivation to resort to political plunder. Houston, in particular, is unique in this respect. It's a one-time phenomenon, growing at a rate never before experienced in this country. Office buildings have been going up at a pace not even conceived of in the good old days of New York. It is the healthiest big-city economy in the country.

The problem is that Houston's very optimism could be its undoing. For the first time in the history of any large city, the greater-fool theory has become a full-fledged, major industry. A whole army of people in Houston buy real estate at higher and higher prices, *based solely on the belief that greater fools will come along and pay them even higher prices.* An acquaintance of mine, Carlo Corleone, has made millions at this game for himself and his investors.

As this book is being written, however, the "recession" is starting to be felt in Houston. The strength of the Houston economy (and the character of its people) could prevent the city from falling as far as others; on the other hand, Houston could experience the worst crash of all simply because it has the greatest distance to fall. One distinct negative consideration is that the city's growth has attracted an influx of voting-class workers from the Northeast and Midwest, and, as a result, city officials are already beginning to babble about "the need to better regulate the city's growth." This, of course, is the economic kiss of death. It will be interesting to see if the hard-core free-enterprise types in Houston have the will to hold their ground.

Obviously, when I talk about western cities, California cities, with the possible exception of San Diego, are excluded. Next to Los Angeles, people in San Francisco are getting California's best view of the collapse of Western Civilization. I heartily agree with Gary North's assessment that if God doesn't destroy San Francisco, he should apologize to Sodom and Gomorrah. I won't bother to discuss Oakland, because most people don't really consider it to be a city. It's so desperate that it's down to trying to confiscate a football team just to keep afloat.

Assuming you have the good sense to consider moving to a smaller city, one of the first things you should check into is the tax structure of any area you may be interested in. Many states, such as Nevada and Texas, do not have income taxes, which can be extremely important if you're in a high tax bracket. Others have no sales or estate taxes. Then there are local inventory taxes, personal-property taxes, and real-estate taxes to consider.

My suggestion is that you write to the Chambers of Commerce in those cities that, on the surface, pique your curiosity, and ask for all the information available regarding industry, taxes, entertainment, climate, and other matters that are of interest to you. Then, after reviewing all the information, you should personally visit those cities that seem most desirable.

All the while, of course, you will want to keep in mind business opportunities, the nuclear map (unless you are totally unconcerned about this danger), and comfort (i.e., primarily climate). I wish I could make the decision for you, but obviously I can't.

Even if you cannot see yourself moving in the near future— maybe the "timing isn't quite right"—at least give yourself the advantage of being mobile. Every day of your life you should do something, no matter how small, to maneuver yourself into a more mobile position. Ideally, you and your family should be able to relocate very quickly to a safer area if all the crazies like The Tortoise, Howard Ruff, and Douglas Casey somehow turn out to be right.

The important thing is to do *something,* beginning right now, even if that means only thinking about the problem. The urban time bombs are relentlessly ticking away. I don't want the satisfaction of being right; I want the satisfaction of knowing that I helped you to avoid a dangerous situation.

WEAPONS

The heart of every self-defense program is a weapons supply. Yes, I'm speaking the unspeakable. I'm talking about buying—horror of horrors—guns. Wow! A media scoop—a red-neck tortoise! It's yahoo time! The Tortoise must be one of those National Rifle Association nuts. On cue, everyone guffaw.

Liberal smart-aleck rhetoric aside, this is an issue where there is no middle ground. While it's true that the Second Amendment to the Constitution guarantees "the right of the people to keep and bear arms," that is not where I make my stand. Even if the Constitution did not make this issue so eminently clear, I believe that it is every individual's *natural* right to defend himself against aggression—whether it be civilian or government aggression. And he has the further right to use any means he chooses to accomplish such self-defense. He can never be in the wrong, no matter what methods he uses, because he is only exercising his natural right to stop someone from committing aggression against him. There can be no compromise when it comes to self-defense.

Gun advocates who argue against gun control on the grounds that it may eventually lead to confiscation of hunting weapons miss the point. Gun advocates who argue against gun control on the grounds that it would increase crime miss the point. Gun advocates who argue against gun control on the grounds that it would require massive paperwork and bureaucratic enforcement measures miss the point. The only relevant issue (aside from the fact that the government doesn't have a right to keep you from owning *anything*) is self-defense. You have a natural right to defend yourself and your family, and it's none of the government's business how you go about it.

From whom do you need to defend yourself? First, the everyday criminals who already roam the streets. Second, the millions of people who will be main-line participants in the social disorder, anarchy, and violence of the future. Third, the government.

While the first two categories are obvious, virtually no one thinks of defending himself against the government. Yet, as people were recently reminded in Poland (by the fact that they had no weapons), a weapon is your last resort of defense against a

"Yahoo!"

tyrannical government. As I said in *Restoring the American Dream*, "the right to bear arms should be defended to the bitter end. Because in the bitter end, as the American Revolutionists discovered, it may very well get down to a matter of whether or not you *do* have arms."

I realize that if things get to the point where government thugs are intent upon smoking you out, your little arsenal may very well be useless. To be sure, in today's world of powerful governments, a person would have to be desperate to resort to such drastic measures. Nonetheless, I would rather have the option of deciding whether or not to implement that last resort if and when the occasion arises, than seal my fate ahead of time by voluntarily disarming myself. Who knows but what the possession of a simple weapon like a handgun could someday be the difference between imprisonment (or death) and freedom?

It is obvious, then, why governments wage continuing battles to disarm their populations. While Washington's nuclear-arms philosophy is "peace through strength," the government expects you to believe that *you* can achieve peace through *weakness*. Has any politician guaranteed to defend you against an intruder who may suddenly appear in your living room? Self-defense is one area of your life where it is especially prudent to be self-sufficient.

The government, in trying to disarm the public, has resorted to the use of *its* most successful weapon—gradualism. For years its approach has been "selective" gun control, or registration, or some other form of temporary compromise. The technique, as always, is two steps forward, one step back—until finally a generation is born that does not question a request to turn in all weapons.

Much to the government's dismay, however, gradualism has not yet produced the hoped-for success in this area. A small but very vocal minority has managed to forge a successful opposition. This being the case, the Big Liars have had to step up their campaign against ownership of guns and are now brushing aside the niceties and going right to the ultimate objective—confiscation of all weapons. Morton Grove, Illinois, was a breakthrough; then the first major city, San Francisco, attempted to follow suit. Soon there will be many more cities, led by liberal councilmen, who will take the same step. Ultimately—and you can absolutely count on this—there will be a federal law against ownership of handguns, and, in addition, probably rifles. As with gold or any other item that the government does not want you to have, threatened future confiscation is the *very reason* you had better make certain that you *do* have guns.

Start laying out your plans for gun ownership *now,* and make your first purchase as soon as possible. On the other hand, if you're planning on buying a gun and just stashing it away on the top shelf of your closet, forget it. You're probably better off with no weapon at all.

What I'm talking about here is the purchase of *many* guns. I'm discussing what liberals like to refer to as "yahoo" stuff, a "John Wayne mentality," or simply "radical-fringe paranoia." I sincerely hope that, just this one time, liberals will practice what they preach, because then you and I won't have to worry about their having guns when chaos reigns over the land. I sure wouldn't count on it, though.

Individual preferences will, of course, vary when it comes to makes and models of guns. However, I would be derelict if I did not recommend that you include at least several .22 caliber and .25 caliber pistols (because of their easy concealment), and at least one or two good .45 caliber weapons (perhaps one revolver and one clip-fed gun). In addition to your array of handguns, you may want to consider something a little more exotic, along the lines of an Israeli-made Uzi or an AR-7 Explorer semi-automatic rifle. Both of these weapons are very accurate at medium range.

If you've never purchased a gun before, you may be overwhelmed by the variety that is available. And you definitely will be overwhelmed by the differences of opinion among gun experts about which weapons are the most accurate, safest, most practical, and easiest to handle. Therefore, *you* will ultimately have to be the judge.

If you've already purchased one or more guns, you are aware

of one major problem. You must fill out a form, which is forwarded to Washington, and from that point on the bureaucratic snoops know exactly which weapon or weapons you've purchased. Rather convenient when it comes time to confiscate them, wouldn't you say?

There are two ways around this. The first is to buy your guns on the black market. This is more expensive, of course, because you're paying the seller for the risk he's taking, but it may be worth the extra money to know that your gun ownership is a private matter. (Eventually, of course, this is the *only* way that you will be able to buy guns.)*

The second alternative is to make your purchases at gun shows. Gun shows are sponsored by private groups, usually several times a year, in all major cities. At present, people are allowed to buy and sell guns secondhand without registering them. This loophole will almost certainly be closed in the not-too-distant future, so if you wish to take advantage of it, you should start inquiring about gun shows in your area right away. You do have to be a little extra cautious when buying a gun from a private owner, because you have no proof that it's in good working order and you receive no warranty with your purchase. As a rule, however, people who are sophisticated enough to display their wares at gun shows take pride in the condition of their weapons.

And, in case you're wondering, the answer is: Yes, *pay cash.* Do not use checks and do not sign anything. We've already been over the paper-trail problem. For the same reasons, keep your gun purchases to yourself. This is one area of your life where it's crucial to zip the lip.

I said earlier that you should not buy a gun and just stash it away on the top shelf of your closet. That's because the last thing in the world you want to be is a one-shot wonder. You sometimes read stories about little old ladies who pulled revolvers out of top drawers and killed intruders the first time they ever fired a gun.

---

*Readers are advised to acquaint themselves with gun-registration requirements in their areas so as not to be in violation of any state or local laws.

Those are heart-warming tales, but, unfortunately, there are many more stories about little old ladies found dead on their living-room floors.

The time to take your first shot is not when you have a human threat standing in front of you. Visit a firing range—frequently. Take lessons. Practice. Know how to use each and every one of your weapons. Know what to do when they jam (sorry to scare you, but they *do* occasionally jam). Be proficient at cleaning them. *Be prepared.*

Now for the finale on self-defense: *You must be mentally prepared to use your weapon against an aggressor.* No matter how much you practice and no matter how well you take care of a gun, if you're not mentally prepared to use it, you may be worse off with it than without it. I hope you never have occasion to use a gun in self-defense, but the rapidly accelerating collapse of our societal structure makes that wish uncertain, to say the least.

The fact is that it's prudent to acknowledge the *possibility* that you may have to use a gun someday. If you can get past that psychological barrier, the next step is to mentally rehearse the hypothetical showdown every day of your life. This is the only way you can be absolutely certain that you will be psychologically prepared to pull the trigger, if and when that unpleasant moment arrives. And when you picture it, don't envision aiming at your aggressor's foot. You should resort to using a gun only because the other person has made it clear that he intends to harm you. Act—and aim—accordingly.

A gun is a means of protecting your life and property from those who would try to take them from you. You never point a gun at someone for any other reason. You never pull out a gun unless you've already made the decision to use it. It is not a toy. It is not a means of threatening someone. It is not for showing off. Though it is socially impolitic to talk about it, the gun was invented for the purpose of killing people. (That is the *only* reason that governments have millions of them.) If you're not ready to kill someone, *don't pull out a gun.* Better yet, don't own one. You'll only end up getting *yourself* killed.

Above all, don't allow yourself to be intimidated by "yahoo" taunts. In truth, it's the gun-control advocates who are the yahoos. For a gun is really a civilized man's ultimate insurance policy against uncivilized men. And a man who carries no insurance is irresponsible.

Violence is already here, and more—much more—is on the way. You may not like to think about options like relocation and weapons, but you would nevertheless be wise to do so. Remember, when I first discussed actions and consequences, I pointed out that even *inaction* is a form of action. If you fail to take action in the area of self-defense, your inaction will have appropriate consequences. How grave those consequences may be is something neither you nor I can know until they occur. But why gamble? Take the initiative and figure self-defense into your long-term planning, *before* the government decides to restrict your options.

SECTION IV

CHANGING TIMES

CHAPTER XI

What We Have Here Is a Failure to Communicate

Chinn Ho, Hawaii's "Chinese Rockefeller," stated in a recent interview, "Time levels, and we are all in its path." His statement reminded me very much of Will Durant's observation, after three-quarters of a century of diligent study, that humility is the first lesson of history.

Man has always tended to take himself and his civilizations very seriously, yet to do so is vain. On the screen of history, Western Civilization, from beginning to end, will ultimately be but a blip. On the cosmic calendar (now about 14 billion years old, give or take a few billion years), it is too insignificant even to record.

I remind you again that the end of Western Civilization does not mean the end of the world. It just means that the world is in a state of flux—*as always.* In reality, every person in human history has lived through changing times. We just happen to be living at a time when the world is changing very rapidly, because at the end of a historical cycle, change tends to accelerate. And while a rapid rate of change may be somewhat unsettling to those living through it, the fact remains that human beings do adapt. It is precisely because of its adaptability that the human race has moved relentlessly forward, century after century, in the face of every conceivable kind of adversity.

213

We are now living in an age that is exemplified by Mr. Bad Dude's running loose on the streets; more specifically, it is exemplified by the fact that Mr. Bad Dude can pretty much do as he pleases. For those of us who can remember a time when the moral structure of Western society was such that Mr. Bad Dude instinctively knew his proper place, adjusting to a new standard of behavior can be quite difficult. Difficult, but not impossible; difficult, but necessary. In our rapidly changing world, an individual who aspires to happiness and financial success *must* adjust.

To make adjustments, one must first acknowledge reality. One must understand that we now live in a world where most people believe that their personal desires constitute legitimate "needs," and that the satisfaction of those "needs" constitutes a legitimate "right." We now live in a world where rudeness, incompetence, and poor workmanship are the norm. Above all, we live in a world that abhors individual sovereignty—a world where envy is the reigning religion of the day.

Once a resourceful individual understands these realities, once he grasps the breadth and scope of the accelerating changes that are taking place, he is in a position to make the proper adjustments and continue forward. The necessary reconciling usually involves little more than common sense. For example, since lynch-mob rule is now morally accepted, it just makes good sense to do everything possible to stay out of the way of the mob. Time isn't the only thing that levels; envious people can also level, but you *don't* have to be in their path.

Instead, make an effort to share a pathway with people who still cling to Western values. True, they are in the minority, yet they still number in the millions. And the best way to attract them is to reflect these values yourself. Honesty, self-sufficiency, self-discipline, an emphasis on nonviolence, respect for the property of others, planning for the future—traits and beliefs such as these are now especially conspicuous to like-minded people. The more you display them, the more likely you are to attract other individuals who are standing right side up.

At the time of the writing of this book, the price-inflation rate in Argentina had hit somewhere between 135% and 400%, depending upon whose figures you chose to believe. While a three-digit price-inflation rate is unfathomable to most Americans, the fact is that industrious people in Argentina continually adjust to it. Those who acknowledge reality, and base their actions accordingly, do just fine. The most resourceful people do better than just fine—they become wealthy as a result of the chaos.

On the other hand, no one becomes wealthier—or happier—by listening to his government's exhortations. Whether in Argentina, Poland, or the Soviet Union, those who make it in life are the ones who do the *opposite* of that which politicians and bureaucrats urge them to do. Remember the premise of this book—that the most certain road to success is to do the opposite of that which causes failure. Take your cue from people who have lived through social and economic collapse in other countries. Throughout recorded history, happiness and financial success have been the rewards of those who have ignored the popular misconceptions of their times and severed their paths from that of the masses. It is within your power to do the same.

Success is possible only to the individual who correctly perceives the way the world works. As I pointed out, people in economically chaotic countries like Argentina, who not only acknowledge reality but base their actions on it, do very well. The qualifier (i.e., acknowledging reality and basing one's actions on it) is all-important. If one allows personal hopes or emotions to enter into his decision-making process, he is unlikely to make sound decisions. It is a noble gesture to carry on the fight for individual sovereignty (a fight that I myself intend to continue), but a wise man will base his plans for the future on the facts. Specifically, he will plan for the worst while hoping for the best.

Understanding and acting on reality is not such an easy task in today's world, because everywhere you turn you are encouraged not to do so. As the saying goes, what we have here is a failure to communicate. It's as though *two* Western worlds now existed. In one world are the people (the vast majority of the population) who insist that everything is going to be just fine (until recently, they insisted that everything *was* fine, but even the staunchest optimists have now given up on that misperception); in the other world are those who point to history, human nature, and the hard facts and conclude that very serious problems are on the horizon.

To further confuse the issue, many of those in the first group claim that most of the problems of Western nations have been *caused* by the negativism of those in the second group! This is tantamount to saying that if someone points out that a building is on fire, his calling attention to the fire either caused the fire in the first place or is making it worse. Truly, this is the kind of logic that one can expect to hear only in a world turned upside down.

The two worlds that now exist, then, are the *real world* and the *unreal world*. Unfortunately, the vast majority of people in Western nations stubbornly choose to live in the unreal world. They choose to live in a world whose problems are expected to disappear just because they want them to or because politicians say they will. In short, they choose to live in a Galbraithian world of fantasies.

If the worst should occur, millions of these people may ultimately see the light and opt for the real world, but for them it may be too late. They may have ignored reality for too long, and, as a result, they may be totally unprepared to live in a world that was unthinkable to them throughout most of their lives. Remember, as a result of the moral revolution, they are, morally speaking, standing on their heads. And the world looks very strange from such a vantage point.

The important thing for you to realize is that *you* have a choice—a choice as to whether or not to end up in the same stew as the unprepared masses. You can, if you wish, choose to live in the real world. You can, if you wish, choose to be prepared, even if every one of your friends and acquaintances scorns such preparation. Don't allow yourself to be intimidated by peer or family pressures. The instinctive thing is to follow the pack; the right thing is to act on the evidence at hand.

In that regard, I hope that this book has served as an important first step for you. My primary intent has been to *mentally* prepare you for the future, because, thus prepared, you are likely to take whatever actions are necessary to be physically prepared as well.

Above all, I hope this book has helped you to answer the three questions I first stated in Chapter 3:

1. What do I want out of life?
2. What will it cost me?
3. Am I willing to pay the necessary price?

At the very least, I hope it has motivated you to begin thinking about them. And, while thinking, keep in mind the realities of today's world and the likely realities of the world of tomorrow. Within that framework, you can very much control your own destiny. Viktor Frankl's words are worth repeating: "Everything can be taken from a man but one thing: the last of the human freedoms—to choose one's attitude in any given set of circumstances, to choose one's own way." Choose, then act.

On that appropriate note, I conclude by wishing you the utmost in health, happiness, and success during the continuing collapse of Western Civilization.

AFTERWORD

Is It Too Late?

I have often been asked if I think it is too late for Western Civilization to be saved. Technically speaking, the question is improperly phrased. Remember, the revolution—the moral revolution—is already over. The shift from a society that once held individual sovereignty sacred, to a desires-are-rights, anything-goes society, is virtually complete.

The more proper question, then, is: Can we, as a people, *re-discover* the morals, ethics, and values that once served as the foundation of Western Civilization? If so, then there is no reason to believe that we cannot experience a rebirth of all that typified the Western way of life.

In my view, the only way that we can hope to rediscover the principles of Western Civilization is to have the courage, wisdom, and insight to recognize the *cause* of its collapse. The reason that solutions offered by politicians, establishment-type academicians, and media "experts" have proven to be useless is that they totally ignore the real problem—i.e., the *moral* problem.

In order to appreciate how deep are the roots of this moral problem, a brief historical background is helpful.

CLASS WAR

Class war—war between the "haves" and "have-nots"—has been a fact of life throughout recorded history, and it is a fact of life today. Yet class war is something one does not talk about in public. It's one of those subjects that is, shall we say, in bad taste—a topic the average person would prefer to avoid.

At its worst, class war manifests itself in bloody revolutions, such as the French Revolution of 1789. At its best, it takes the form of a "cold war," such as that which has existed throughout most of the history of the United States. But, hot or cold, *class war always exists.*

The human emotions that fan the embers of class war are covetousness, greed, and envy. Plain and simple, the have-nots want what the haves possess. If they cannot rise to that level of affluence, then the least to which they aspire is to drag the haves down to their own level of misery. The latter desire, as Gary North has pointed out, constitutes a philosophy of destruction. If a person believes that he can never hope to achieve the level of success he sees others enjoying, he sometimes finds comfort in seeing their possessions and achievements destroyed. Or, as Tocqueville noted, "There exists also in the human heart a depraved taste for equality, which impels the weak to attempt to lower the powerful to their own level, and reduces men to prefer equality in slavery to inequality with freedom."

When I speak of haves and have-nots, I am referring to the two most clearly definable classes in any society—upper and lower. Occasionally, however, a large "middle class" has evolved, such as has existed in Western nations during most of this century. In such a case, much of the middle class, like the lower class, ultimately comes to envy the upper class and covet its wealth; the lower class has designs not just on the upper class, but on the middle class as well. This casting of envious and covetous eyes on those above one's station in life never stops; it only varies in intensity from country to country and generation to generation.

By and large, of course, nothing ever changes, relatively speaking, for the lower class and much of the middle class. (I am speaking here of classes in general, not of specific *individuals.*) I use the phrase "much of the middle class," because a majority of the people in today's middle class are misplaced. They are merely lower-class people who have effectively used the government's lynching mechanism to gain false entrance into the middle-class camp. One of the good things, then, about the collapse of our legalized system of theft is that it is forcing the nonproducing members of the middle class—those who have achieved their status through artificial means—back into their proper slots in the lower echelon of society. The true producers of the middle class, of course, should not be affected over the long term.

Two things, however, do change for the lower class and much of the middle class: the faces of the political powerholders who control their lives and the system that is used to control them. In Poland, for example, a familiar scenario has been repeated during the past couple of years. Workers have embraced the illusion that if only Lech Walesa could be their leader, through the machinery of a labor union, all would be rosy for them. Alas, they understand neither politicians nor the laws of nature.

Nature will always separate human beings into strata according to such characteristics as ability, ambition, intelligence, and determination. And politicians, no matter how convincing they may seem, are interested, first, foremost, and always, in *power.* Whenever a Lech Walesa has successfully charged to the frontlines of power on his white steed, history has recorded little change in the lives of the proletariat.

Even when changes have taken place, they have for the most part been temporary. What has happened in Western countries during the past fifty years is a perfect example of this. The moral revolution that removed the underpinnings of the West was, for the masses, perhaps the most successful revolt in history, in terms of both the quality and duration of its benefits. Having as its springboard the reassuring guise of a political democracy, and evolving over a long period of time, its primary achievement was in gradually benumbing producers, whose potential rewards were great, into sharing increasingly greater portions of their earnings with nonproducers. Thus, producers pressed on in the face of ever more grandiose and onerous government schemes to carve up the fruits of their labor. As a result, the millions of peasants on the receiving end, particularly in the United States, have temporarily been privileged to own suburban homes, drive new automobiles, dine out regularly, and take vacations never before dreamed of by nonproducers.

These same proletarians now see their unearned good life slipping away, piece by piece, and they are, quite understandably, both frightened and angry. Morally and economically un-enlightened, they now believe, tragically, that they are *entitled* to these things. As I watch the laws of nature and economics rudely putting them back in their proper places, I am reminded of the words of Benjamin, the donkey, in George Orwell's classic, *Animal Farm*: "Windmill or no windmill . . . life would go on as it had always gone on—that is, badly." The masses are simply returning to their natural way of life—a bad life.

Even if one were to argue that some people at the lowest end of the income ladder are better off after so-called socialist revolutions, the reality is that such people give up virtually all freedom in exchange for guarantees of a cheap roof over their heads and a few crumbs of food each day. After 6,000 years of recorded history, the hands of power still continue to change, but the plight of the uninformed, naive masses stays pretty much the same.

What in fact usually happens in a successful revolution is that a new upper class emerges. The doors of elitism swing open and new *individuals* (i.e., a small number of people, as opposed to the masses as a whole) rush to take their places inside, as Alvin Toffler describes in *The Third Wave*:

> Time and again during the past three hundred years, in one country after another, rebels and reformers have attempted to storm the walls of power, to build a new society based on social justice and political equality. Temporarily, such movements have seized the emotions of millions with promises of freedom. Revolutionists have even managed, now and then, to topple a regime. Yet each time the ultimate outcome was the same. Each time the rebels re-created, under their own flag, a similar structure of sub-elites, elites, and super-elites.

Basically, there are two methods for holding the masses at bay: repression and bribery. Obviously, these are the antithesis of one another.

Machiavelli, in advocating repression, never intended to be a moralist, just a pragmatist. In substance, he was merely underscoring the cliché, "If you give them an inch, they'll take a mile." Unfortunately, he was right. Whatever else one might think of Machiavelli, one must admit that he did understand human nature.

But repression of the masses is not always so easy as it appears, as dictators like the Shah of Iran, Somoza of Nicaragua, and Batista of Cuba found out. A dictatorial regime must know how to run a tight ship. Some have done just that and have managed to last for decades, even centuries. In this century the Soviet Union must be given the palm for excellence in the art of repression. After sixty-five years, its people are still under the tight control of the oligarchical Politburo. Its secret, like that of all successful repressive regimes, is that it is so brutal and efficient in crushing individual rights that the early smolderings of a revolution are never given the opportunity to begin.

At the other extreme is bribery, a method whereby the haves, in effect, attempt to buy off the have-nots with government largess. This approach is not peculiar to Western Civilization. It has been tried—always unsuccessfully—many times through the ages. Will Durant's *Caesar and Christ* is most insightful in this regard. Durant explains how, in 494 B.C., large numbers of plebeians in effect went on strike, proceeding to the Sacred Mount on the river Anio, just outside of Rome. They insisted that they would not work or fight for Rome until certain demands were met, one of the most important being to cancel or reduce their debts. The Senate finally agreed to their demands, thus beginning a long and familiar history of governments and producing classes yielding to the demands of the masses. From that point on, there was a continuous stream of men, like Spurius Cassius (486 B.C.), Spurius Maelius (439 B.C.), and Marcus Manlius (384

B.C.), who were forever trying to distribute wheat, land or other commodities to the "poor" in exchange for "votes."

In more modern times, the graduated income tax has been the device most useful in quenching the thirst of envy. The failure of this bribery mechanism to endure for the long term is attributable, as one would expect, to human nature. On the one hand, the greed and envy of the nonproducer is insatiable, so that eventually nothing short of 100% taxation will appease him. On the other hand, long before a level of total confiscation is reached, producers begin to figure out what is happening, which results in tax evasion, emigration, rebellion, black markets, and a refusal to work. And that leads to the rather awkward problem of there being no wealth available to distribute to *anyone,* which in turn precipitates violence and accelerates the collapse of the societal structure.

Because both repression and bribery are delicate arts for keeping the have-nots in place, governments are constantly gyrating between the two. Left-wing dictatorships, while controlling the masses through brute force, like to create the impression that they are benevolent. However, the skimpy food and minimal shelter they provide their citizens, along with the miserable and/or nonproductive jobs they force upon people, are but a charade. State workers in Poland are governed by the rule: "Whether you stand up or lie down, you get paid just the same." Or, as one worker put it, "The government pretends to pay us a wage, and we pretend to work."

POLITICAL DEMOCRACY

How does America's way of life—a political democracy—fit in with the historical realities of class war? As practiced in the real world, the nature of a political democracy opens the door to the ultimate bribery scenario. The problem is that the have-nots, educated through the government's mass-education programs, become experts at the ballot-box game.

As a result, they no longer wait to be bought off. Instead, they begin to *dictate* the terms of the buy-off by lynching the haves through the political system. And, in exchange for holding office, politicians willingly agree to carry out the lynchings, or forced buy-offs, on behalf of the voting class.

This is the political reality that assures that all government-proposed solutions will, at best, be short term and cosmetic. No politician dare attack the real problem. To tell the recipient of a forced buy-off that his little game of desires-are-rights is immoral would be political suicide. Have you ever heard even the most conservative elected official tell his constituents that our problems are a direct result of the covetousness, greed, and envy of voters? Yet, until people understand this truth, a renaissance of Western values cannot begin.

To comprehend just the fiscal seriousness of a desires-are-rights, anything-goes society, consider this: It took 186 years for the federal budget to reach $100 billion (in 1962), but only nine years for it to reach $200 billion; it took just six years for it to double to $400 billion, and it now looks as though it will reach $1 *trillion* within eight years. The interest alone on the national debt is now greater than the entire budget was just twenty years ago— *and climbing.*

The picture that these exponentially increasing figures clearly paint is one of a public that is hooked on a legalized system of plunder. What makes it even worse than drug addiction is that it has entrapped a *majority* of the population of the Western world. Unfortunately, there is an inherent desire in men to prosper without effort. And it is the very *repression* of this desire, both voluntary and through the institution of laws, that makes a civilized society civilized.

But as Western Civilization's collapse has accelerated, its legal system has been turned upside down. It now *sanctions*—in fact, *enforces*—the taking of others' property. Wealth without work is now encouraged by the power structures of *all* Western countries. And since it is only natural for men to want to avoid hardship, while at the same time enjoying the good things in life, the masses are not about to let go of their something-for-nothing cornucopia without a fight. Having been sold on the egalitarian illusion that their desires can be fulfilled through the use of force, they desperately fear any proposed change in the lynch-mob-rule structure that has, until recently, filled their consumption cup to the brim. Sadly, then, the average person has a *short-term vested interest* in perpetuating the present system. Each individual perceives that he is a beneficiary of government laws and programs.

But it is not just the masses that stand in the way of a return to a moral society. As paradoxical as it may seem, big business, whose leaders are entrenched members of the upper class, now fully support the plunder system arm in arm with the proletariat. Why? Because major corporations, having adjusted their financial planning and product designs, as well as their marketing strategies, to a theft-is-moral society, have a large stake in seeing to it that the rules of the game remain unchanged. Were it not for continued inflation, taxation, government subsidies, plunder laws, and other forms of government intervention in the economy, many large companies would simply cease to exist. At the very least, they would cease to be large.

Take the banking industry, for example. Banks benefit very directly from the redistribution schemes, because a large percentage of the money that government creates is created through the banking system. The more leeway banks are given to inflate their supply of "money," the more they can "earn" on money created out of thin air (i.e., they are allowed to earn interest on money that does not really exist).

But bankers are not alone in syphoning off the earnings of producers. Entire industries have grown up on a foundation of monetary inflation and redistribution laws. Where would Las Vegas be if a whole generation of Americans had not been made to feel much wealthier than they were? Thirty years ago, Las Vegas was a haven for well-heeled people who wanted to get away for a few days and relax. Now that the wealth has been spread around through force and fraud, Las Vegas no longer caters just to the few who would really be able to afford it in a free society, but to the masses, most of whose pockets are lined with unearned dollars.

Millions of people, who as recently as twenty or thirty years ago would no more have thought of flying to Las Vegas to give away hundreds, or even thousands, of their (at that time) hard-earned dollars to the blackjack or crap tables, now flock there even in the worst of times. If the United States suddenly reverted to a totally free society in which each individual was allowed to keep 100% of what he earned, and could receive no more than what an employer was willing to pay him without government coercion, and if the government was taken completely out of the money business, both Las Vegas and Atlantic City would collapse overnight.

How about the fast-food industry? Or the hotel/motel industry? For some time now, the name of the game has been to gear your products and services to society's lowest common denominator. You don't build Holiday Inns and cook Big Macs for "the rich." All major corporations now cater to the masses, because that's where the big dollars are. Just appeal to the lowest common denominator, and you have it made.

On top of these unfortunate realities of our lynch-mob system of redistribution, the whole problem is exacerbated by the liberalist media, which continually incite the public's envy. How right Tocqueville was. Envy was the backbone of the moral revolution and is the driving force that is used to keep the new moral standards in place. It is all too easy for the liberal media to stir up the irrational hatreds of millions of people, who see themselves as less fortunate than others, by repeatedly talking about the billions of dollars in "windfall profits" earned by major corporations, by featuring periodic stories on the opulent living of wealthy individuals, or by pointing an accusing finger at "loopholes" used by "the rich."

In these troubled times, in particular, it is quite natural for the average person to feel a sense of frustration over his financial problems. And the perfect fix for such frustration is the appearance of a scapegoat. The media, in an ongoing campaign to win votes, gladly provide such a person with just that. They imply that it is "the rich" who have oppressed him. The liberal's poisonous rhetoric has an implicit message that goes something like this: "There is only so much wealth that exists on earth (a foundational lie), and you are being deprived of your fair share by greedy people who have far more than they need." Presto—the have-not is given an outlet for his frustration. Oh, how good it feels to hate!

Thus the process feeds on itself. The more envy, the more destruction; the more destruction, the less there is to buy off the envious; the less the envious receive, the more they envy. It is a closed loop of destruction.

For the liberal, guilt is the handmaiden to envy. While the have-nots march to the media's envy tunes, the haves are easy targets for guilt-based manipulation. It is no wonder that the middle class is the biggest loser during these turbulent times. As the false prosperity of middle-class people continues to disappear, they feel more and more frustrated, and therefore increasingly vulnerable to envy-provoking media stories. Yet, at the same time, the media subtly encourage them to feel guilty for living so much better than the lower class! The middle class is thus beset with both envy *and* guilt!

The systematic manipulation of guilt is so important to the modern political structure that Gary North contends that without such manipulation, the entire structure would collapse. He points out that by passing mountains of laws (most of them directly concerned with confiscation of income), it becomes virtually impossible for people not to "break the law" in their normal course of living. Through subtle media urging (sometimes not so subtle), friends and neighbors constantly admonish people for not abiding by the rules, and such people usually oblige by feeling guilty.

Apparently shameless, the media have found that they can use the same guilt ploys over and over again without experiencing a backlash. One such staple features bright-eyed, smiling youngsters happily eating their taxpayer-subsidized lunches. If someone dares to suggest that perhaps the poorest of mothers could afford to make sandwiches for her own children in order to shave a billion dollars or so from the budget, he is scorned and accused of being cruel and heartless. The guilt-loaded, implied question is, "Would you deprive these innocent little children of their minimum daily nutritional requirements?" Never does an interviewer ask how children managed to survive before such a program was instituted. It wasn't that long ago that a suggestion that government might someday provide school children with daily lunches would probably have elicited the traditional, naive response, "Oh, don't be silly. Things will never get *that* out of hand."

Thus, the enormity of the problem is quite obvious. With the voting class addicted to the good life, big business addicted to the profits of a theft-is-moral society, and the media addicted to the thrill of concocting its poisonous brews of guilt and envy, how can an elected official possibly tell his constituents the truth? The person who is best positioned to do so is the president of the United States, yet we have already seen the futility in a president's trying even to make vague references to the real problem.

When it comes right down to it, President Reagan, like all presidents before him, unfailingly backs away from the moral issues. While espousing freedom and free enterprise on the one hand, Mr. Reagan reassures the nation on the other that his budget cuts will not include programs that would affect "the truly needy." In reality, such assurances simply mean that he is guaranteeing that the anything-goes game will continue unabated.

But even if a president were willing to attack the real root of the problem, he is helpless to do so. The reason is the federal-budget phenomenon of "uncontrollables." These include Aid to Families with Dependent Children, unemployment compensation, food stamps, Medicare and Medicaid, and, above all, Social Security. Not only are these programs not being cut by any significant amount, if at all, but all of them have *automatic cost-of-living increases built into them.* Thus, even if a president had the *courage* to declare war on these plunder programs, he would not have the *power* to do so. Yet these thefts alone comprise 75% of the federal budget!

To grasp just how fully the forces of gradualism have won out—how totally the desires-are-rights mentality is entrenched—one must juxtapose the miniscule impact of President Reagan's proposed redistribution cuts against the public's reaction. For example, in 1981 the President proposed removing 875,000 people from food stamps at a savings of $1.6 billion. This would still have left the food-stamp budget at a figure more than *68,000%* greater than it was when liberal proponents first pushed it through as a harmless measure to help a few "truly needy" people. The President also proposed removing 400,000 families from the Aid to Families with Dependent Children program and reducing the benefits of another 287,000 families at a savings of $1 billion a year. This still would have left the budget for this program more than *28,000%* greater than what it was in its first year (1935), when its purported purpose was to assist widows with children. (Today, 80% of all AFDC payments go to mothers whose husbands have *deserted.*)

The reaction to these proposals? Among other things, some 260,000 people marched on Washington to protest President Reagan's "meat-axe" approach to cutting the budget. And, of course, the liberal media have continued to label him heartless, cruel, and "insensitive to the needs of 'the poor.'" Based on this, try to imagine what the reaction of the masses would be if a president made a *serious* attempt to cut the budget—say, by one-half? Or three-quarters? The reality is that such cuts are politically impossible in today's environment.

The bribery approach has worked well for politicians, and they are not about to stop using it to their political advantage. Thus, they unashamedly continue to fan the fires of class war, and, as a result, our political democracy continues to mushroom into out-of-control buy-off programs. Long term, however, bribery does not work in a society founded on a political democracy, because people's desires are infinite. What happens is that covetousness, greed, and envy ultimately destroy a nation's wealth-producing capacity. On the surface, this appears to be a pragmatic problem; at its heart, however, it is a *moral* problem. This is why no establishment solutions work; they fail to address the *moral* issue. At the very least, the solutions currently being proposed are based on the status-quo notion that if a person desires something, he has a *right* to it—by using whatever means necessary. To be sure, not one politician, not one media commentator, not one public figure has thus far dared to attack the real problem.

SOLUTIONS

In light of the foregoing discussion of class war and political realities, the question again presents itself: Is it too late for Western Civilization to be saved? Or, more properly, can we, as a people, rediscover the morals, ethics, and values that once served as the foundation of Western Civilization?

To answer this question, I am going to examine four possible solutions, three of which are among those most commonly offered or implied. The fourth is rarely discussed, and, on those rare occasions when it does get a hearing, the crux of the issue is unfailingly ignored.

The Muddle-Through Solution

If you've ever had the experience of listening to an otherwise knowledgeable and rational person insist that he is optimistic about the future of Western Civilization, without giving any concrete reasons for his optimism, you were probably listening to someone who, perhaps unknowingly, was relying on the Muddle-Through Solution.

The Muddle-Through Solution transcends all facts and logic simply by maintaining that Western man will "somehow" work out his problems and manage to muddle his way through. Times may get terrible; inflation may destroy currencies; there may be rioting and bloodshed in major cities; but, through it all, the re-silient Western man will manage to patch up the cracks and pre-serve the Western world intact.

I am often tempted to take the easy way out myself and turn to the Muddle-Through Solution for solace. What is attractive about this idea is that it enables one to rid his mind of the multi-tude of seemingly insurmountable negative facts that presently point toward a police-state environment, without taking the pains to analyze their causes. Whenever I find myself starting to believe that we might just manage to "muddle through," I force a return to reality by asking myself a one-word question that refuses to be ignored: *How?* And the answer is that there is no way to return to a moral society without *specific action.* The problem with the idea of muddling through is that it's a *no-action* solution, which means it ignores the manifold egalitarian realities that already exist. To be sure, life will go on if we muddle through, but not in the man-ner to which we have become accustomed.

I have previously expressed my belief that, as our system continues to disintegrate, millions of people who have come to believe that their handouts are "entitlements" are going to be very upset, to put it mildly. To put it not so mildly, they are going to become violent. And uncontrolled violence leads to a dictator-ship—*always.* So-called democracies are simply too inefficient to suppress violent nationwide uprisings.

Unfortunately, the vast majority of the population believes in redistribution of income and assets, thus the demagogue most likely to succeed in grabbing the reins of police-state power will be an FDR-type personality—i.e., a committed left-winger who is eloquent in getting across his redistribution promises. (Lest you need reminding, people do *not* "muddle through" under left-wing dictatorships. Wherever you look for an example—the Soviet Union, Cuba, Ethiopia, Nicaragua—dictatorships that were cleverly masked as "people's revolutions" have been eminently successful in keeping people under both mental and physical lock and key.)

The attempt to muddle through will only mean more and more "stopgap measures" to keep the thousands of government giveaway programs from collapsing. It will mean an increase in covetousness, greed, and envy, and the total reliance of non-producers on the effectiveness of lynch-mob rule. Charades like "supply-side economics," periodic announcements that "Social Security can and will be saved" [Ronald Reagan—December 1, 1981], increases or decreases in the federal discount rate, and the institution of a "negative income tax" will not only continue to fail, but will make matters worse. The reason they will fail is because none of them addresses the real problem.

On the contrary, all of them avoid the *moral* issue. They do absolutely nothing to abate the envy of the masses. Instead, they rely on ever-increasing doses of bribery, and, since the productive capacity of those who continue to produce is limited, are destined to fail. If a majority of people continue to rely on the Muddle-Through Solution as the answer to Western Civilization's collapse, you can be sure that the future will continue to look bleaker and bleaker. The Muddle-Through Solution is the only "solution" that has virtually no chance of succeeding.

The High-Tech Solution

The theory behind the High-Tech Solution is that mankind is now on the threshold of scientific and technological advances so enormous in scope that the producers of the Western world will soon be able to fulfill the desires of even the most greedy non-producers.

Geniuses in electronics, medicine, ocean-floor farming, and many other important areas are hard at work on projects that could dramatically upgrade our way of life. Once their techniques are perfected, there will be such an abundance of food, housing, medicines, and even the luxuries of life, that they can be made available to everyone—including the laziest, most incompetent, and most ignorant people in society.

While such talk is capable of fostering hope in the most pessimistic of minds, I still find it difficult to avoid referring to this theory as the High-Tech Pollyanna Solution. I have the utmost faith in science and technology, but it's human nature that tempers my optimism. The success or failure of this alternative really boils down to the answers to two questions: 1) Will the hoped-for offspring of science and technology arrive *before* the onset of a dictatorship, a dictatorship that would, at the very least, drastically retard the rate of scientific and technological advancement? 2) Human nature being what it is, will nonproducers *ever* be satisfied, regardless of how many free goods and services they receive as a result of widespread technology? My heart answers these two questions with a hopeful "yes," but my powers of reason, leaning heavily on history and human nature, tell me "no."

Again, the High-Tech Solution skirts the central issue. Instead, it promises only to be a super buy-off of the masses. It does nothing whatsoever to help forge a new moral structure; on the contrary, it merely whets the appetite for unlimited wealth without work.

The Selfish-Gene Solution

The Selfish-Gene Solution is discussed only behind closed doors, and then only by the most extreme right-wing conservatives.

Richard Dawkins, in his candid and sobering book, *The Selfish Gene*, scientifically explains the futility of the liberal's drive for an altruistic society. In genetic terms, he dissects why it is literally impossible for any living organism to act altruistically. Benevolent rhetoric aside, the fact is that the process of natural selection assures that an organism *must* act selfishly in order to survive.

This does not mean that it must harm others in the process (although most living creatures do so). It does, however, mean that every living thing will act in its own best interest at all times. Fortunately, it is possible for the most advanced living organism—Homo sapiens—to do this without aggressing on the rights of others.

Though undoubtedly very few right-wing conservatives have read Richard Dawkins, they are, unknowingly, relying on his self-ish-gene explanation to save civilization. I have heard such people opine that, when things get out of control, the power structure, no matter how liberal its public utterances, will come down on the side of law and order, property rights, and a free market. In the end, they say, the masses will be repressed instead of bribed, be-cause the financial power structure will never allow a left-wing dictatorship. They will not allow it because, at the moment of truth, they will do whatever is necessary to assure their own sur-vival.

In fairness to those who believe in this solution, one must admit that there have been a handful of right-wing dictatorships that have worked out reasonably well for producers. Spain, under Franco, is a recent example. During Franco's tenure, Spain was a safe, clean place to live, with plenty of opportunities for ambitious people. While those who were repressed would strongly disagree, Franco's results made a strong case for the "benevolent right-wing dictatorship," if there can indeed be such a thing.

Nonetheless, I would abhor any kind of dictatorship, be it from the right or left. Aside from the obvious immorality of dic-tatorial repression, the Selfish-Gene Solution, like the first two solutions, does nothing to resolve the destructive and immoral de-sires and emotions of the masses. It merely represses these emo-tions, thus encouraging them to privately smolder and pose a revolutionary threat.

The Mass-Education Solution

To my way of thinking, there is only one solution that speaks to the very heart of the problem, without violating anyone's rights. It is what I refer to as the Mass-Education Solution. Since the cause of the collapse of Western Civilization was a moral revolution, it seems logical to assume that the rise of another Western-style civilization can be brought about only through a new revolution—a *moral revolution*. Such a revolution would have to be diametrically opposed to the notion that a person is automatically entitled to anything he desires.

What I am talking about here is nothing short of mass *moral education* of the public. A person does not genetically inherit morals; he acquires them. And, unfortunately, he presently acquires them, to a great extent, through the public-school system. To rediscover the morals, ethics, and values that once served as the foundation of Western Civilization, the majority of people in Western society must be *reeducated*. They must be taught to reject the belief that it is moral to violate the rights of others simply by outvoting them. They must be taught to see the fallacy in the currently unchallenged premise that anything a majority decides is automatically moral. They must be taught that individual sovereignty is the most sacred right of every human being.

This will not be an easy task, because, through the decades, collectivists have given teeth to the moral revolution by translating their immoral objectives into law. Along with this clever inversion of morals, people have been taught to believe that something is moral just because it is "legal"—and they are continually admonished to be "law abiding." Thus, plunder is accepted as moral simply because it is decreed and sanctioned by law.

Through the deployment of gradualism, the egalitarian philosophy has been so ingrained in our thinking that it subtly pervades every area of our lives. Nowhere is it more prevalent than in movies and television. For example, in the movie *Star Trek II: The Wrath of Khan*, Spock's dying words, presumed to be gallant, are: "The needs of the many outweigh the needs of the few—or the one." This kind of brainwashing today enjoys such widespread acceptance that one refuses to conform only at the risk of being ostracized by friends and associates. What kind of morals, ethics, and values can a youngster be expected to have when he grows up hearing such uncivilized mumbo-jumbo day in and day out?

Even in sports, equality of results is considered to be a noble objective. The National Football League, for example, long ago instituted a perverse system that rewards losers and penalizes winners. Last-place teams choose first in each year's draft and are awarded the easiest schedules. On top of that, they share equally in television revenues, no matter how badly they perform.

This subtle erosion of a once-cherished moral structure has been so successful that it has caused an even greater problem than the mental contamination of the masses: It has soiled the minds of prominent individuals who are basically freedom and free-market oriented. This in turn exacerbates the problem of educating the masses, because the freedom and free-market advocates most visible to the general public base their arguments on a status-quo foundation. In other words, they do *not* zero in on the moral issue. To a man, they seem to agree that the best solutions are those that are "best for the greatest number of people." Which is just another way of saying: *anything goes.*

Prime examples of this are the most widely known "free-market" economists, or so they are labeled by the liberal media. Take Arthur Laffer, whom the general public perceives as an up-and-coming free-market whiz. His claim to fame? Mr. Laffer argues that if the government would just lower its income-tax rates, consumers would spend more and companies would invest more in production. As a result, personal and corporate income would rise, and taxes, in turn, would *increase.* This is Laffer's case for a free market—a scheme to help the government steal *more* from the public than it is presently able to extract. Challenging theft as an *immoral action* never enters Laffer's arguments.

Another young darling of fiscal conservatism is George Gilder, author of the book, *Wealth and Poverty.* Among other things, Gilder insists that a "capitalist" is motivated primarily by altruism—that his real desire is to help others, and, as a by-product, he ends up making profits for himself. If I were at the lower end of the income scale and heard this explanation being proffered by a conservative economist, I, too, would hate capitalists— for insulting my intelligence!

There's more. Gilder has publicly stated that "a reduction of inflation to zero is probably undesirable." He has also explained that a function of the banking system, to a considerable extent, is to borrow short and lend long. He notes that, as a result, people periodically discover that the banks have no money in them and they react with horror. He concludes, however, that "that situation does not alarm me much."

Then there is the most publicized of all conservative economists, Dr. Milton Friedman. Dr. Friedman is primarily known for his "monetarist" approach to economics. He believes that the government (through the Federal Reserve system) should "fine tune" the money supply, and, by so doing, better control the economy. Great—if you're a collectivist! *But free-market economists are not supposed to want the government to control the economy—or anything else.* A *true* free-market economist just wants the government to get out of the way!

The sad reality is that Dr. Friedman is not against the government's counterfeiting of money. His only argument centers around how much counterfeiting it is *practical* for the government to undertake at any given time. As a result, he blames the Federal Reserve Board for prolonging the depression of the 1930's, because it did not print up fiat money *fast enough* to pump up failing banks.

And, like Messrs. Laffer and Gilder, Dr. Friedman never argues the immorality of taxation. Instead, he suggests only that present welfare programs should be superficially altered and that "the poor" should be subsidized through a "negative income tax." As though a theft by any other name is not a theft!

Worst of all, Dr. Friedman has an annoying habit of prefacing his discussions of liberals and their redistribution programs with statements like, "There's no question that these people are well-meaning and have nothing but good intentions, but ...." This has led to more specific apologia like, "The objectives (of HEW) have all been noble; the results, disappointing." The ultimate blasphemy in this respect came in his television series, "Free to Choose," when he commended Franklin D. Roosevelt for some of the emergency measures he instituted during the depression.

All of these supposedly brilliant men seem to believe that the moral justification for capitalism is that "the poor," or, at least, "the greatest number of people," are better off under its workings. But that is not a moral justification; it is a *rationalization.* The moral justification for capitalism is that men—all men, no matter how rich or how poor—*have a right to be free.* All men have a right to trade their goods, services, and labor for any price they can secure in a free market, without interference from the government or anyone else, and all have a right to keep *100% of what they earn,* no matter how small or how great those earnings may be. Freedom from *all* forms of coercion is a moral objective, *regardless* of whether or not it helps others.

Put more bluntly, what you earn and what you own is nobody else's business, including and especially the government's! This is what individual sovereignty is all about. People must learn that privacy is a moral objective. Certainly it is a civilized objective, as Stephen Rinehart has pointed out: "Civilization is the process toward a society of privacy. The savage's whole existence is public, ruled by the laws of his tribe. Civilization is the process of setting man free from men."

What we are talking about here is the *crux of the education issue.* People must be taught that only *voluntary* compassion is moral; *compulsory* compassion is coercion. And coercion is *always* immoral. Liberals like to insist that anyone who is against government handouts lacks compassion. In point of fact, one has nothing to do with the other. The most compassionate people I know are strictly opposed to the use of force (*including* the use of force for the purported purpose of helping "the truly needy"). To stress this point, I borrow my own words from *Restoring the American Dream*:

> While the needs and desires of certain individuals may constitute a legitimate concern to many people, they nonetheless fall outside the scope of man's natural rights. This *does not mean* that men should not be concerned about other men; it *does not mean* that men should not be sympathetic toward

other men; it *does not mean* that men should not be helpful to other men; it *does not mean* that men should not be charitable toward other men. What it *does* mean is that men do not have the right to *force* other men to be concerned, sympathetic, helpful, or charitable toward others.

Explained more simply by Frederic Bastiat, the purpose of the law is not to be philanthropic; it is to protect people's property.

A very wise man once observed that to get at the right answers, we have to start asking the right questions. That indeed is a very big problem today. Because of the success of the moral revolution, virtually everyone now bases his arguments on false premises. To turn things around, a public that has been brainwashed for decades would have to learn to disregard a myriad of fallacious premises that are practically sacrosanct. Only then would it be intellectually free to ask the right questions.

To emphasize the difficulty in such a turnabout, people would have to ask not, "Is majority rule best for the greatest number of people?" but, "Is majority rule, as it is now practiced, *moral?*" They would have to ask not, "Does the present tax structure really help the people it is intended to help?" but, "Are taxes *moral?*" They would have to ask not, "Is enough effort being put forth to cut waste from the federal budget?" but, "Why must there be a federal budget *at all?*" They would have to ask not, "What should the government do to solve this problem?" but, "Why should the government do *anything?*"

Ultimately, if mass education in morals is to succeed, prominent spokesmen must have the courage to say to the masses: "You, my friends, are entitled to *nothing.* You are not entitled to a car; you are not entitled to a job; you are not entitled to medical care; you are not entitled to a roof over your head; you are not even entitled to three meals a day. What you *are* entitled to is exactly what you can *earn* in a free market—or what others are *voluntarily* willing to give you."

Obviously, this kind of frankness will take a great deal of courage on the part of freedom advocates, because the sad reality is that the vast majority of people want *more* benefits, not fewer. Worse, they have absolutely no understanding of either the moral ramifications or the economic consequences of their actions.

"But," you may ask, "what's the use of becoming involved in a mass-education program when you've already assured me that we're headed for many years of hard times?" To be sure, the odds are overwhelming that the kamikaze mission of fiscal suicide I referred to in an earlier chapter will have to be carried to its final conclusion before people will even consider listening to "radical" solutions. What is not certain, however, is *which* radical solution they will listen to.

Keep in mind the most likely scenario: While a 1930's-style deflationary depression is possible, it is highly improbable. It is far more likely that the lethal mixture of covetousness, greed, envy, and political expediency will result in a runaway inflation, and hence a total breakdown of law and order. And, when that happens, you will have the answer to your question.

What do I mean? Simply that, when chaos overtakes our society, unless the general public is well educated in both morals and economics, they may very well follow some socialist demagogue down the road to collectivist enslavement. That's when the words of Edmund Burke will weigh most heavily: "The only thing necessary for the triumph of evil is for good men to do nothing." Meaning that the idea is to begin to educate people *now*, so when the final breakdown comes they will have the knowledge and understanding necessary to reject solutions that will lead to the loss of their remaining freedoms.

Aside from specific libertarian organizations you can join, such as the Cato Institute in Washington, D.C., you can make a major contribution to the cause of freedom in three ways: 1) by reading the works of laissez-faire authors; 2) by giving copies of these works to friends and associates; 3) by encouraging others to do the same. However, this chain-letter approach cannot be a short-term fad. The Mass-Education Solution requires more than just a few months of concentrated enthusiasm. At this late stage of the game, there can be no letup.

My primary contribution to this cause was the writing of *Restoring the American Dream*. From the outset, I had two objectives in mind. The first was to write a book that emphasized the *morality* of liberty, rather than the *practicality* of liberty. The second was to write a book that could be easily understood. *Restoring the American Dream*, which was published in 1979, has been read by perhaps a million or more people, which sounds very encouraging relative to other books of its kind. But that number is insignificant compared to what must be achieved if education of the masses is to become a reality.

I believe that to even begin to make a dent in the problem, at least fifty million Americans must read a book like *Restoring the American Dream*. To help achieve this end, I have formed the National Committee to Restore the American Dream, the objective of which is to distribute millions of copies of *Restoring the American Dream* at a price slightly above the cost of printing. (If you are interested in becoming involved in this project, you may obtain further information by contacting: National Committee to Restore the American Dream, 220 Montgomery Street, Suite 440, San Francisco, California 94104.)

One word of caution. When soliciting others to help in a mass-education program, be prepared for a great deal of frustration. Not only are most people apathetic, but even those who most fervently believe in freedom and free enterprise are rarely willing to back their beliefs with either time or money. Frank Chodorov, in his wonderful book, *The Income Tax*, poignantly noted this unfortunate truth when he wrote:

> If, for instance, those who prate about "free enterprise" were willing to risk bankruptcy for it, even as the men of the Declaration risked their necks for independence, the present drive for the collectivization of capital would not have such easy going. Assuming that they are fully aware of the implications of the phrase they mouth, and are sincere in their protestations, the fact that they are unwilling to suffer mortification of the flesh disqualifies them for leadership, and the case for "free enterprise" is hopeless.

In simple terms, what Chodorov really was saying was: If capitalists are unwilling to put their money where their mouths are, then the case for freedom and free enterprise is lost by default. And that, in the final analysis, is where the issue will really be decided. *Can* we, as a people, rediscover the morals, ethics, and values that once served as the foundation of Western Civilization? In the end this question will be answered by the answer to another question: Will evil triumph because good men did nothing?

Acknowledgments

I would like first to acknowledge Garet Garrett, whose book, *The People's Pottage,* originally put the idea in my mind that the moral revolution had already come and gone. Second, I am grateful to Gary North for his remarkable insight into human nature. It was through Gary's newsletter, *Remnant Review,* and his book, *Successful Investing in an Age of Envy,* that I really began to appreciate the role envy has played in the political and economic free-for-all that has rocked the Western world. Finally, I wish to thank my good friend, Douglas Casey, for helping me to see the economic consequences of a world gone mad. It is hard to imagine that any individual in this country has a better economic understanding of how the world works. His two most recent books, *Crisis Investing* and *Strategic Investing,* are financial-advice masterpieces, as is his monthly newsletter, *Investing in Crisis.* Because of Doug's uncanny accuracy, he has all but taken the excitement out of the art of economic forecasting.

Above all, I wish to thank those who played key roles in the production of this book. Lynn Michelson is a word-processing master who, throughout this long project, continually pointed out significant errors and made important suggestions, a large number of which I adopted. Carla Honig was instrumental in the editing of the earlier drafts of the manuscript, which only someone with a great deal of courage would have agreed to tackle. Craig Kitson's precision and detail in all aspects of the research was remarkable, and I quickly learned to have complete confidence in his accuracy.

As usual, I will end with my editor, Ellen Shahan. After eleven years and four books, I am running out of superlatives with which to shower her. I have already called her organized, thorough, and brilliant, and have made it quite clear that I consider her to have no equal in her field. It now occurs to me, however, that if such lavish praise continues unabated, my readers may begin to think that I'm overstating my case. You may, in fact, be wondering if an author's relationship with his editor can really be that rosy.

Whoever said anything about its being rosy? I never accused Ellen of being Mary Poppins; I just said she was a brilliant editor. How would you like to have *your* work scrutinized, year after year, by an unmercifully competent grammarian? I tell you, this is a cruel, callous woman. She would not hesitate to cut the last comma out of an already bruised and battered author, then thrust an exclamation point through his heart as he was uttering his last poorly constructed sentence.

So now you know the truth—what *really* goes on behind closed doors. Since a picture is said to be worth a thousand words, I thought I would end this book with an unretouched photo of one of our friendly little editorial sessions.

"All right, all right! You can leave the comma in."

Bibliography

"An Exclusive Interview with Dr. Henry Jarecki, Chairman of Mocatta Metals Corporation." *Silver & Gold Report,* Mid May 1981.

Bartlett, Bruce. "Of Windfalls and Bailouts." *The Libertarian Review,* March 1980.

Baruch, Bernard M. *Baruch: My Own Story.* New York: Henry Holt and Company, 1957.

Bastiat, Frederic. *The Law.* Translated by Dean Russell. Irvington-on-Hudson, New York: The Foundation for Economic Education, 1979.

Bernstein, Harry, and Eaton, William J. "260,000 Protest Reagan Policies." *Los Angeles Times,* 20 September 1981.

Casey, Douglas R. *Crisis Investing: Opportunities and Profits in the Coming Great Depression.* Los Angeles: Stratford Press, 1980

————. *The International Man.* Alexandria, Virginia: Kephart Communications, 1978.

————. *Strategic Investing.* New York: Simon and Schuster, 1982.

"Chief Justice Says Lawyers Charge Too Much." *Los Angeles Times,* 9 January 1982.

Church, George J. "Backing Down on Benefits." *Time,* 12 October 1981.

Chodorov, Frank. *The Income Tax: Root of All Evil.* Old Greenwich, Connecticut: The Devin-Adair Company, 1954.

Clayton, Bruce D., Ph.D. *Life After Doomsday.* Boulder, Colorado: Paladin Press, 1980.

Dawkins, Richard. *The Selfish Gene.* New York: Oxford University Press, A Galaxy Book, 1976.

Durant, Will. *Caesar and Christ.* New York: Simon and Schuster, 1944.

Durant, Will and Ariel. *The Lessons of History.* New York: Simon and Schuster, 1968.

Eaton, William J., and Irwin, Don. "Reagan's Budget Cuts Spare Social Programs." *Los Angeles Times*, 11 February 1981.

Farnsworth, Clyde H. "Budget Plan Would Raise U.S. Debt to $1,250 Billion." *The New York Times*, 7 February 1982.

Fialka, John J. "Disability-Claim Cases Under Social Security Are a Boon to Lawyers." *The Wall Street Journal*, 14 January 1982.

Fixx, James F. *The Complete Book of Running*. New York: Random House, 1977.

Frankl, Viktor E. *Man's Search for Meaning: An Introduction to Logotherapy*. Part One translated by Ilse Lasch. New York: Washington Square Press, 1963.

Friedman, Milton and Rose. *Free to Choose*. New York: Harcourt Brace Jovanovich, 1980.

Friedrich, Otto. "F.D.R.'s Disputed Legacy." *Time*, 1 February 1982.

Garrett, Garet. *The People's Pottage*. Caldwell, Idaho: The Caxton Printers, Ltd., 1965.

Gilder, George. *Wealth and Poverty*. New York: Basic Books, 1981.

Gillette, Robert. "Black Market in Gasoline Costing Moscow Millions." *Los Angeles Times*, 25 January 1982.

Hayek, Friedrich A. *The Road to Serfdom*. Chicago: The University of Chicago Press, 1944.

Hill, Napoleon. *Think and Grow Rich*. North Hollywood, California: Wilshire Book Company, 1966.

Hillinger, Charles. "Guarding the Country's Gold at Ft. Knox." *Los Angeles Times*, 17 April 1980.

Holley, David, and Jameson, Sam. "Using a Lawyer in Japan Is Embarrassing." *Los Angeles Times*, 29 October 1978.

Hopkins, Claude. *Scientific Advertising*. New York: Crown Publishers, Inc., A Chelsea House Book, 1966.

Hospers, John. *Libertarianism: A Political Philosophy for Tomorrow*. Los Angeles: Nash Publishing, 1971.

"IBM Antitrust Lawsuit Filed in '69 Is Dropped by U.S.; AT&T Settlement Begins Six-Year Revamping Process." *The Wall Street Journal*, 11 January 1982.

Irwin, Don. "Will Save Social Security, Reagan Tells Aging Parley." *Los Angeles Times*, 2 December 1981.

Jackson, Brooks. "Mergers Are Set for 2 Failing S&Ls; Cost to U.S. Agency Is Called Substantial." *The Wall Street Journal*, 2 June 1981.

Jastram, Roy W. *The Golden Constant*. New York: John Wiley & Sons, A Ronald Press Publication, 1977.

"Jim Cook Interviews George Gilder." *IRI Insights*, March–April 1981.

" 'Keep the Faith'—Carter." *Los Angeles Times*, 9 June 1980.

Kempe, Frederick. "Poles Survive Collapse of Currency by Using Own System of Barter." *The Wall Street Journal*, 23 October 1981.

Larson, Erik. "Why Do Some People Outperform Others? Psychologist Picks Out Six Characteristics." *The Wall Street Journal*, 13 January 1982.

Lochte, Dick. "Tale of Hailey's Comet." *Los Angeles Times*, 29 February 1976.

Machiavelli, Niccolò. *The Prince*. Translated by George Bull. Baltimore, Maryland: Penguin Books, 1961.

Martinez, Al. " 'Chinese Rockefeller'—He's a Legend in Hawaii." *Los Angeles Times*, 23 May 1982.

"Miami Schools Reopen; 5 Police Are Suspended." *Los Angeles Times*, 22 May 1980.

"Miami Violence Leaves One Dead, 7 Hurt." *Los Angeles Times*, 29 December 1982.

Monahan, Jane. "Ruiz Mateos: Wealthiest Man in Spain, Architect of an Empire Called Rumasa." *The Wall Street Journal*, 30 November 1981.

Morgan, Lael. "Path of Suicide Taken by Rising Number of Youths." *Los Angeles Times*, 28 February 1980.

Myers, C. V. *Money and Energy: Weathering the Storm*. Darien, Connecticut: Soundview Books, 1980.

————. *Myers' Finance & Energy*. No. 295, 4 January 1980.

Noble, Kenneth B. "Conferees Clear Bill to Shore Up Savings Industry." *The New York Times*, 30 September 1982.

North, Gary, ed. *Remnant Review*, 16 May 1980.

————. *Successful Investing in An Age of Envy*. Sheridan, Indiana: Steadman Press, 1981.

Ogilvy, David. *Confessions of an Advertising Man*. New York: Atheneum, 1980.

Orwell, George. *Animal Farm*. New York: New American Library, A Signet Classic, 1974.

Paine, Thomas. *The Age of Reason*. Secaucus, New Jersey: Citadel Press, 1974.

"Poland: A Three-Class Society." *Time*, 1 September 1980.

"Prime Raised to 21½% But Bond Rates Decline." *Los Angeles Times*, 20 December 1980.

Prugh, Jeff. "15 Dead in Miami; Rioting in 2nd Night." *Los Angeles Times*, 19 May 1980.

Pugsley, John A. *The Alpha Strategy: The Ultimate Plan of Financial Self-Defense*. Los Angeles: Stratford Press, 1981.

Rich, Spencer. "U.S. Pays High Price to House the Poor." *Los Angeles Times*, 28 August 1980.

Rinehart, Stephen. "Freedom or Altruism." Mimeograph of a manuscript outline, 1981.

Ringer, Robert J. *Looking Out For Number One*. Los Angeles: Los Angeles Book Corp., 1977.

————. *Restoring the American Dream*. Los Angeles: QED, 1979.

————. *Winning Through Intimidation*. Los Angeles: Los Angeles Book Publishers Co., 1974.

Rosenblatt, Robert A. "75% of Outlays Go for 'Uncontrollable' Benefits." *Los Angeles Times*, 29 January 1980.

Ruff, Howard J. *How to Prosper During the Coming Bad Years*. New York: Times Books, 1979.

————. *Survive and Win in the Inflationary Eighties*. New York: Times Books, 1981.

Russell, Bertrand. *Why I Am Not a Christian*. New York: Simon and Schuster, A Touchstone Book, 1957.

Russell, Richard, ed. *Dow Theory Letters, Inc.* Letter 804, 11 March 1981.

Sahagun, Louis. "Computers on Hot Roll and Parts Pay Off." *Los Angeles Times*, 18 January 1982.

Schumacher, Edward. "Argentines Groan at Mind-Boggling Inflation." *The New York Times*, 26 August 1982.

Schuster, Lynda. "Many in Nicaragua Who Aided Sandinists Now Resent Their Rule." *The Wall Street Journal*, 15 January 1982.

Science of Success and the Art of Prudence, The. Translated by Lawrence C. Lockley. San Jose, California: University of Santa Clara Press, 1967.

Seeger, Murray. "Rapidly Changing Gold Scene Stirring New Debate Over Metal's Role." *Los Angeles Times*, 27 February 1980.

Simon, William E. *A Time for Action*. New York: A Reader's Digest/Berkley Book, 1980.

"Statistical Abstract of the United States, 1981." U. S. Department of Commerce, Bureau of the Census, 102d Edition.

Stone, Marvin. "Our Hungry Lawyers." *U.S. News & World Report*, 13 November 1978.

Sullivan, George, ed. "The Most Significant Changes in the Past 10 Years." *TWA Ambassador*, July 1978.

Sutton, Antony C. *The War on Gold*. Seal Beach, California: '76 Press, 1977.

"Time to Spare the Rod in Sweden." *Los Angeles Times*, 31 May 1979.

Toffler, Alvin. *The Third Wave*. New York: William Morrow and Company, 1980.

"Troubled Teenagers." *U.S. News & World Report*, 14 December 1981.

"World Currency Authority Dr. Franz Pick Now Believes—'The Dollar Will Be Wiped Out; the U.S. Will Issue 1 New Dollar for 100 Old Ones.' " *Silver & Gold Report*, A Special Report, 1980.

Index

252